# When to
# Call a Therapist

# When to
# Call a Therapist

Robert C. Ciampi, LCSW

Editorial work and production management by Eschler Editing
Cover design by Natasha Brown
Interior print design and layout by Marny K. Parkin
eBook design and layout by Marny K. Parkin

Published by Scrivener Books

ISBN 978-1-949165-12-8
First Edition: July 2019
Printed in the United States of America
10 9 8 7 6 5 4 3 2 1

 # Contents

 Acknowledgments

I would like to acknowledge to the people listed below, for their help and support in the writing of this book. To the many clients I have worked with over the years who entrusted and shared their life stories with me. Without you, this book could not have been written. My friend and colleague Margaret Debrot, LCSW, Psy A., with her experience as a writer, provided thoughtful insight and encouragement throughout the process of publishing my book. Giacomo "Jim" Giammatteo, author, who advised me telephonically, by email, and through his blogs on so many areas of the writing and publishing process. Thank you! To Kate Colbert, owner of Silver Tree Publishing, for editing my manuscript early on and for guiding me through the publishing process by email and videoconferencing. You pointed me in the right direction from the very beginning. To the many professional social workers at the National Association of Social Work New Jersey (NASWNJ), who guided me with answers to my questions regarding social-work policy and ethics. Your advice has always been appreciated! To Tammy Smith, LSW, psychiatric social worker, for reading sections of my nascent book and also providing feedback and support in the process. To Natasha Brown, author, for working closely with me in helping to develop my cover design. To the folks at Eschler Editing—Angela Eschler, Chris Bigelow, Michele Preisendorf, Shanda Cottam, and Melissa Dalton—for your expertise in helping me make this vision a reality.

 # Introduction

For many, making the first appointment with a therapist is an anxiety-producing experience. Questions like the following come up quite frequently.

- ◉ Who do I call?
- ◉ Should I get a referral from someone I know?
- ◉ How do I know if therapy can help me?
- ◉ Should I tell my family and friends I am going to see a therapist or keep it private?
- ◉ Am I ready to make this kind of commitment?
- ◉ How long will I need to be in therapy?
- ◉ Should I work with a male or female therapist?
- ◉ Can I trust spilling my feelings to a stranger?

And "When should I start therapy?" As we will see throughout this book, getting into therapy should start *much sooner than later* in order to make needed adjustments before relatively benign issues can turn into deep-seated problems.

Therapy can fall under a number of different names: psychotherapy, counseling, marriage-and-family therapy, social work, substance-abuse counseling, licensed professional counseling, coaching, psychoanalysis, and more. Therapists can work with many different populations, such as children and adolescents, adults, substance abusers, the developmentally disabled, the elderly, and forensic clients. And therapists can practice with numerous different modalities, including cognitive-behavioral therapy (CBT), dialectical-behavioral therapy (DBT), solution-focused therapy, eye-movement desensitization and reprocessing (EMDR), family-systems therapy, twelve-step programs, and many other types and subtypes of helping therapies.

A common question people ask is "What is the difference between a therapist, analyst, counselor, social worker, psychologist, and psychiatrist?" The short answer is that therapy is a category of psychology practiced by mental-health professionals who are trained differently and have specialties and degrees other professionals may not have. For example, substance-abuse counselors are trained in alcohol and drug abuse, social workers and clinical social workers can work in many different settings (i.e., schools, hospitals, mental-health-care facilities, government agencies, etc.), with many licensed clinical social workers also in private practice. Psychologists have a PhD in a defined area of focus and are trained to perform psychological testing in many different settings. Analysts are trained to look at clients' characterological issues. And psychiatrists are medical doctors who primarily prescribe medication in various settings. With so many therapists and their different titles and roles, it's no wonder why "getting into therapy" can be a daunting task.

**Getting Started**

Where can potential psychotherapy clients find a therapist? Some people start with a search engine like Google to research nearby therapists. Others search specific sites, such as *Psychology Today*, which list therapists along with a brief biography about their style of therapy and the populations they serve. Word of mouth, or a recommendation from a friend or family member, is another way people learn about a therapist. Another health-care professional, such as a physician, can refer a patient to a therapist if they feel their patient can benefit from the psychotherapy process. And a person can go online to their health-insurance-company site to find an in-network provider. These are the most common ways to connect with a therapist, but ultimately it will be the client-therapist relationship that proves most important. More on this later.

American society has come a long way in diminishing the stigma of having emotional, psychiatric, or substance-related problems and needing to seek help. However, the fear of others knowing that a person is in therapy or the thought that they must have a "weak character" and cannot handle their own problems is still a barrier for many. And, unfortunately, this barrier may preclude people from embracing the help they need in order to live a more contented and productive life. Fortunately, there are many stigma-free programs being initiated in municipalities, in counties, on college campuses, and elsewhere, with the hope that many more individuals will reach out for help without fear of being labeled for an illness they suffer with in silence.

This book should be read by anyone thinking about calling a professional therapist for help. With therapy, many become aware of how their skewed thinking patterns, poor communication styles, anger, sadness, anxiety, substance abuse, lack of decision-making abilities, and that feeling of being "stuck" can negatively affect their life. Some problems are multifactorial. For example, a married couple with poor communication skills who argues regularly about their chronic financial problems may find it affects their intimacy. Various issues need to be worked through by the client and therapist to enable the client to make a better decision about any conflicts weighing on their mind. Still other problems are more complex, like substance abuse and eating disorders, where not only would it be beneficial to be in individual therapy but also a higher level of care such as a program, meetings, and possibly medications or hospitalization.

The purpose of this book is to help individuals get a sense of *when* they should enter therapy. It has been my experience that many people, especially couples, start therapy way too late. Often, with marital counseling, couples decide to enter therapy as a last-ditch effort to save their marriage only to find that the process should have been started much sooner. Those suffering from anxiety wait until they have built compensatory coping strategies for their fear and panic that have stopped working for them. Substance abusers are often in denial and cannot admit they have a problem until they hit "rock bottom," which can come in the form of legal problems, loss of employment, loss of relationships, or an overdose. And those suffering from prolonged depression may not have the energy to call a therapist, which can have deadly consequences. It's bewildering to me that some clients say they will get into therapy or back to therapy when they are feeling better. I have heard clients say, "I'm feeling too anxious to come to therapy right now" or "I'm too sad over my divorce to come in" when, in fact, this is the exact time to schedule an appointment. This counterintuitive thinking can get in the way of feeling better. Getting into therapy *sooner* than later can give many individuals the time they need to work through their issues before those issues become serious problems.

Please note: This book is not meant to assess, diagnose, or treat anyone with medical, emotional, or psychiatric problems. If you are experiencing any serious physical or mental-health issues and believe you need help, either go to your nearest emergency room or call 911 immediately.

# Chapter 1

# My Story

## *Why I Believe Therapy Will Help*

Years ago, when I was in my twenties, a friend suggested I reach out to a therapist to talk about what was going on in my life or, more aptly, what was not going on. I was stuck trying to figure out what to do and which direction I wanted to go in life. I was anxious, depressed, and confused as to whether I should settle for a secure "regular" job with good benefits, as my father wanted me to do, or dare to have higher aspirations and build a professional career. After graduating high school, I did not have plans for college, nor did two of my high school buddies. The thought of not having much to do that summer did not sit well with me. One of my friends came up with the idea of driving across the country to see his brother who was in the air force in California and had an off-base apartment, where my friend was planning to stay. Another friend had been invited and joined suit, and then I was invited. After some haranguing with my parents to let me go, the three of us hopped in a Chevy van and were off. For me, this was going to be the beginning of a journey, literally and figuratively, in finding my way in life. I was going to the West Coast to "find myself," as did many other seekers in the 1960s and 1970s. The trip itself was wonderful. My friends and I discovered what a vast and beautiful country we have, with so many various points of interest. From the cornfields of Indiana, to the Rocky Mountains in Colorado, the Pacific Ocean and Mohave

Desert in California, and the Grand Canyon in Arizona, I knew I would be a different person when I returned home. Several weeks later, back to New Jersey we went, filled with tales about our trip. But after the photographs were developed and the adventures discussed, there was reality staring me in the face again. What did I do now? And where were all those answers I was hoping to find on the trip?

I started working a succession of odd jobs, but nothing meaningful came of it. I did some house painting, helped my girlfriend's parents set up antique shows in malls, dabbled in some retail work, and was given a job by a relative driving luxury cars off the New Jersey docks into New York City. It was fun for an eighteen-year-old, but it didn't last long. It seemed like everyone around me was offering suggestions as to what I should be doing, but I had little interest in what they were saying. Eventually I found work as an ID checker in a bar, then graduated to bartender. That job was fun, fast-paced, loud, and high energy, everything a late teens–early twenties person would want. Making quick tips and getting paid "under the table" wasn't a bad deal either. Eventually, after doing that for a couple years, I decided to look for work that would earn me a steady paycheck in a less chaotic environment. I found a job in a retail wine store and began to feel as though I had finally landed and had the structure I was looking for: eight-hour days, five days a week, regular paychecks, and an environment where I learned a considerable amount about wine. Here I had a "following" who would come in to see me for my wine selections, which did a lot for my ego. With friends, colleagues, and customers who became friends, I put together wine tastings, wine dinners, went to tastings with the owners and winemakers of established wineries, and did just about everything that could include wine. I even worked my way up to wine manager—a proud achievement. Life was good. However, I knew deep down that this was not my future. As much respect as I received from the customers and the satisfaction I derived from teaching new staff members about the wine business, there were still issues I wasn't addressing—issues regarding my parents and family, relationships, self-esteem, anxiety and depression, not to mention the financial struggles that ate away at me incessantly. I developed ailments, such as stomach issues, IBS, what I thought was a "brain tumor," anxiety attacks, fatigue, and other "conditions" that could not be diagnosed by the many doctors I visited. Spiritually, I was lost. I didn't know who I was and felt I had no purpose. I felt direction-less, confused, and was numb to life. This was particularly frightening because, at times, I was sure I didn't exist at all.

At this point, a friend of mine started to push me toward calling a therapist, but my anxiety increased with the pressure to do so. My friend had already been in therapy and found much of it to be a good experience at a time when he was having increased anxiety after he'd left a position at an Ivy League university and started a family of his own. Therapy, for him, was a way to work through his anxiety and helped him change his angst into more positive thinking patterns. If it had helped him, he believed, it would help me too.

I began searching for a therapist close to home and was amazed at how many therapists there were in my hometown. I jotted down several of the names I found through various resources (there was no Google at the time) and began to call them. With most, I did not make contact directly but was given the option to leave a message. Since my anxiety was so high, I do not remember leaving a message for anyone. I just hung up the phone. But one day I called a therapist on the list and was surprised when someone actually answered the phone. It was one of the therapists at a counseling center who identified the center he was calling from and then asked in a calm and steady voice, "How can I help you?" Since my anxiety was so high, I was barely able to get the words out. I remember saying something like, "Hi . . . I'd like to get some information on the counseling center." I waited for a response. The person at the other end of the phone politely asked me what kind of information I was looking for, which put additional pressure on me to come up with another response. I told the person I was thinking about making an appointment to see a therapist but was not sure how the process worked. The voice told me about the center and said there were several therapists who worked there. He indicated that he was one of the therapists and asked me what had prompted me to pick up the phone and call. Again, I wasn't sure how much to divulge, and so I just explained how I wanted to find direction in life and was unsure where I wanted to go and how to get there. The therapist felt he could help me and asked if I would like to set up a time to meet. I froze and felt put on the spot, and I remember saying something like, "Thanks for the information. I'd like to think about it, and I will call back." In a soothing voice, the therapist said he understood that I may not be ready and that I could call whenever I would like. I ended the call and for a while sat introspectively, wondering if therapy was something I really wanted to pursue. The idea of entering therapy increased my anxiety, but the thought of not trying to work through my issues also fueled that anxiety. I seemed caught in the middle. I let my friend know that I had called but did not feel ready to make a commitment yet. He seemed to understand and congratulated me for at least making the call. I felt like something in me was changing.

Several weeks passed, and I called the counseling center again. This time I did leave a message with my home phone number. Surprisingly, a short time later, the phone rang, and the same therapist I'd spoken to weeks prior was on the line again. After a brief conversation, I was again invited to set up an appointment, and again I indicated I was not ready for that. We ended the call with the therapist reassuring me I could call back anytime. I felt bad I had called the counseling center a second time and still not made an appointment. I was worried the therapist would think I was playing a game and really wasn't interested in therapy. Now, in addition to my general anxiety, I was beginning to have self-doubts about my sincerity to begin the process. This weighed on me for about another week, when I called a third time and made an appointment for the following week. I felt relieved in the moment, but I obsessed about the appointment and worried about the upcoming session.

I had my first appointment the following week. I felt plenty of uneasiness and trepidation about what therapy was all about, and I was skeptical of what I could gain by going, but the therapist was a kind and gentle person who saw how anxious and depressed I was. He guided me expertly through the process each week, and I always left the sessions feeling relieved and empowered. After some time, I sensed I was becoming a new person. As the sessions continued, I was starting to feel less anxious and depressed. I seemed to have more confidence, was worried less about what others thought, and was starting to make requests of others, something I had never done before. Also, I remember being validated for the progress I had made, which made me feel like a "worthy and good" person, and in my dull, black-and-white view of the world, I started to see some color.

I liked my therapist because he was real. He was nonjudgmental in his guidance and would tell me when I was going down the wrong path, but he would also reward me for the progress I made. I began to feel that this was the right decision at the right time for me, and those closest to me noticed my growth. As I became stronger, a few people wondered what was different about me as evidenced in the way I now interacted with others. I began to question everything I knew, including the people, relationships, and direction I was going. At times, my world felt upside down as I left my "comfort zone," but, as they say, change occurs when the pain of not changing is greater than the pain of trying something new. I became excited by what I was going to learn next and what "secrets" I would uncover about myself in the next session. What I discovered was that I was a complete and whole person, but based on the circumstances and skewed perceptions I'd developed in my life, these positive qualities had been eclipsed by anxiety, low self-esteem, and depression.

Years of therapy help me reshape my thinking and persona, which led me to having the courage to enter college and excel in all of my courses. For a while, I was in both individual as well as group therapy, where I received feedback from a broader group of people, which also added to my growth. And later, because I found therapy so help-ful, I added couples counseling with the woman I was living with at the time. I was seeing my therapist for individual therapy one to two times a week and going to group therapy once a week. Then, when my eight-year relationship with my girlfriend started to unravel, we began couples counseling once a week. That was a lot of therapy; however, in retrospect, it was a necessary part of my overall growth and progress. The relationship did not survive, but before it dissolved, I was enrolled in college and on a path that would change my life in ways I never dreamed. It was a long haul, burdened not only by the breakup but also by the fact that our shared condo was going into default. Even with what appeared to be losses at the time, I later realized that these were necessary losses—aspects of my life I needed to jettison in order to move forward. When everything was said and done, I'd not only com-pleted my bachelor's degree in psychology, I'd also finished my master's in social work. I was on my way and had my friend to thank for steer-ing me in the direction of therapy, which ultimately changed my life.

Therapy helped transform my life and point me in a direction I may not have otherwise gone. It's scary to think what path I might have taken if not for those who were instrumental at that point in my life. Sometimes I lament the fact that I was a "late bloomer" and that I should have begun my journey earlier in life. It worked out for me in the end, but my advice to others now is do not delay. Tackle your problems *sooner than later* so you avoid not only the time wasted but also the pain that delaying the necessary work often brings.

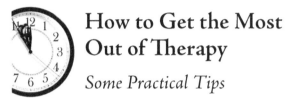

# Chapter 2

# How to Get the Most Out of Therapy

*Some Practical Tips*

Many "high profile" individuals in the sports, music, and entertainment world have gone public about their mental-health and substance-abuse issues. Their courage is not only cathartic for them but the beginning of destigmatizing the problems many others suffer with in silence. As a society, we are all affected by the struggles of those around us. Mental-health and substance-abuse issues show no regard for affluence or the lack of it, or for race or religious and socioeconomic status. Perhaps those reading this book will come to believe that if the superstar athlete or the music sensation can verbalize their need for help, maybe they can too.

This book is designed to help people recognize the signs and symptoms of mental-health and substance-abuse issues in themselves, a loved one, or anyone else they know having difficulties coping with life. This book is laid out in a way that the reader can go directly to an individual chapter, such as the one on anxiety, to become better educated in that particular area. Some may suffer from what's referred to as co-occurring disorders; that is, two distinct issues that occur simultaneously (i.e., a person who lacks assertiveness skills may also be experiencing anxiety). If this is the case, the reader can focus on those particular chapters.

We'll cover the most common mental-health issues that affect people today. Chapters and diagnoses may overlap depending on the circumstances in your life. Reading multiple chapters may be the most useful approach, depending on your particular situation.

## Understanding How Therapy Works

Therapy is experienced differently by different individuals. There is no magic wand in therapy to quickly and easily fix all problems. Instead, therapy should be seen as an investment in yourself with benefits revealing themselves as the process unfolds. A couple of questions to ask yourself at this point may be:

- ◉ Why am I thinking about getting therapy at this time?
- ◉ What do I hope to get out of therapy?

The timing of starting therapy can be helpful for both you and your therapist. This question "Why am I thinking about getting therapy at this time?" more than likely will be asked by the therapist to get an understanding as to what might currently be going on in your life. But it may also give you time to reflect on "Why now?" as well. The timing of you getting into therapy can often ascertain the degree or seriousness of your problems.

"What do I hope to get out of therapy?" may sound like a simple question. You may have tough decisions you are trying to make and would like to discuss your options with a therapist. You may have goals you want to achieve and would like direction in getting started. You may need support in trying to tackle an addiction. Know that your decision to get into therapy may not necessarily be caused by a terrible or serious event. Perhaps today is just the day you decide to make the call to get relief from your nagging, time-worn symptoms. It doesn't matter how you arrive at therapy as long as you get there *sooner* than later.

The therapist you select will have their own style and training. In order to get the most out of the process, the relationship between you and your therapist should take priority. Without a mutually respectful and trusting relationship, one in which you feel safe divulging your innermost thoughts and feelings, the therapy process will be superficial at best. Only when you do not feel judged and that the problems you present are being taken seriously can you truly open up and discuss your fears and concerns. You need to feel you are being heard and understood. An astute therapist may repeat what you say to get a better understanding of your unique circumstances. This allows the therapist to work with clarity and effectiveness. It is also a good indication that the therapist is invested in completely understanding your concerns. Two more questions to assess the therapeutic bond may be:

◉ Is the relationship with my therapist a good fit?

◉ Do I feel comfortable sharing the intimate details of my life with my therapist?

Ask yourself these questions shortly after starting therapy. Do you have a sense that you and your therapist can work closely together concerning your issues? Does your therapist make you feel at ease in discussing your concerns? Therapy is a two-way street with mutual dialogue occurring during the course of the session. It is important that you and your therapist are both vested in the outcome of your work together to get the best results. As the therapy progresses, these questions may come to mind:

◉ Do I feel my therapist has the experience needed to help resolve my issues?

◉ Do I believe my therapist has the proper skill level in order to guide me?

Another important factor in the therapy process is the knowledgebase of the therapist in relation to your particular issues. Many therapists have a lot of training and experience, but no one is a specialist in all areas. This can be discussed in the initial session when you present the problems for which you are seeking help. If your issues are outside the scope of the training of the therapist, he or she should make that known and offer you a referral to a therapist with more experience. You have decided to seek therapy in order to learn coping skills, to discuss a difficult decision to be made, or to feel better in general. That can't happen if you don't feel your therapist understands your situation or is well trained enough to work with you on your particular problems. Chances are you will establish a connection with your therapist right away. However, if for some reason you don't feel like it's a good fit, it's better to take the time to discuss this with your therapist as opposed to just dropping out of treatment. Leaving therapy abruptly may put your progress on the back burner. Even if you decide to seek out other therapy options, I recommend being open and honest with your therapist throughout the treatment process.

## Client Responsibility

Therapy sessions are usually scheduled just one or two times a week, so you will be with your thoughts and feelings many more hours outside the therapeutic environment. Therefore, it is important that you practice the skills learned in the sessions and engage in introspection (the ability to sit and think about what transpired in the sessions) prior to subsequent sessions. Being motivated to feel better will be invaluable to you, not only in the face-to-face interactions with your therapist but in your time outside therapy as well. Motivated clients are better invested in the therapy process and progress faster. Ultimately, the client is responsible for their own healing. Therapy is hard work and is a nonlinear process. Invariably, there will be many steps forward, but also some back. This is part of the process. The more you work on your issues on your own and the stronger you become, the more you'll feel a sense of accomplishment. And with each accomplishment, another "step" will have been climbed on your way to reaching your goals. This is the growth you will notice, where greater confidence and self-esteem are established.

## That "Aha" Moment

Therapy is a synergistic process between you and a licensed professional. Over the years in my private practice, I have found that by sharing the stories of others who've dealt with similar problems, along with their successes, clients often find motivation and hope, even in seemingly hopeless situations. Clients have often told me they've had what is called an "aha" experience when they least expected it. An "aha" moment usually occurs outside the therapy session when a client's eyes are opened to a truth for which they have been searching. It is like finding the missing piece to a puzzle and can be awe-inspiring and even life changing. In my work, I often build on this experience as the therapy process continues.

Therapy is akin to making a commitment such as you would a diet. It usually is born out of feeling "sick and tired" of being sick and tired. Carrying mental-health or substance-abuse issues around is exhausting. It fatigues the body, mind, and soul and can engender a sense of helplessness and hopelessness. There are ups and downs in any commitment, so don't be discouraged if you feel you have fallen back into old patterns and behaviors. Learning from them is key to making adjustments and moving forward. Not everyone's issues are the same, but their problems are their problems, and many people turn to therapy for help. Making a commitment to feeling better and to lead a healthier life is just a phone call away.

## A Sanctuary

A therapeutic environment has been described by some as a "sacred" place. It should be a comfortable and safe space unlike any other place where you can talk about your issues. Where else can you get the attention of an objective, nonjudgmental person where confidentiality is assured? Many clients have told me they have confided in family and friends only to see their issues become more complicated. Families have been splintered, "secrets" revealed, and friends lost over "advice" that may have not been in the person's best interest. This is what makes the clinical environment so special. In order to maintain the integrity of the therapy process, I would like to list what I will call "clinical interrupters" that can get in the way of any progress that has been made:

- ◎ **Setting up your appointment**—If you call your therapist and do not reach him or her directly, leave a clear message so a return call can readily be made. Repeating your phone number a second time is a good idea.

- ◎ **Keep your appointment**—Outside of a true emergency, therapy sessions should not be cancelled, as to do so can have a negative effect on any progress achieved. Also, not showing for a session and not calling the therapist is a clinical issue and should be discussed in the next session.

- ◎ **Avoid distractions**—In order to keep focus in the therapy session, cell phones and electronic devices should be turned off. (In the case of a potential emergency, let the therapist know your phone will be on at the beginning of the session.)

- ◎ **Therapist guidance**—Although the session is yours, allow the therapist to provide structure. Initial paperwork should be completed and questions may be asked so that the therapist can get a better understanding of the clinical issues.

- ◎ **End of session**—With a cue from the therapist, let the session wind to completion. Avoid "door-knob confessions," or bringing up important information as you are walking out the door. Sensitive issues should be discussed at the beginning of the session, not at the end. The clinical dynamics of exiting "revelations" should be discussed in the next session.

- ◎ **Completion of therapy**—It is imperative you do not leave therapy suddenly. There is a therapeutic process for termination, and leaving abruptly before the clinical process has been completed can damage your progress.

Therapy is a special commitment that can help minimize or elevate troubling issues in your life. It is a professional, confidential, nonjudgmental, and uplifting experience that can truly be life changing. Most people experience a sense of relief right after setting up the appointment and report feeling better as they get into their treatment.

## Medication Questions

In some cases, a discussion about medication may arise. The therapist will explain how medication for depression, anxiety, and other mental-health disorders can benefit the therapeutic process and help reduce symptoms sooner. This is your decision to make. Clinical social workers and other therapists do not prescribe medication; that requires a referral to a psychiatrist for an assessment to determine if medicine is indicated. As a client, questions as to what to expect from medication can be explained by the doctor and therapist. Often the therapist and doctor will work together as your "treatment team," with the therapist being the eyes and ears in between appointments with your doctor. It provides a sense of comfort for many to know that they are in the care of two mental-health professionals.

Medication will only work if taken as prescribed. Many medications need to build up to a therapeutic level in your system to be effective. Taking the medication erratically, such as missing days or stopping the medicine without telling your doctor, will not benefit the process. Any side effects from the medication should be reported to your therapist or doctor so an adjustment can be made or a new medication prescribed. It is well documented that the combination of pharmacological treatment and therapy produces the most beneficial effect. If your treatment providers feel this route is most helpful to you, have a discussion, ask questions, and make an informed decision based on any answers given. In my many years of practice, I have seen near miraculous transformations in clients who have decided to take medicine for their symptoms. Medication is not indicated for everyone, but it is another "tool" that can be used to ease debilitating symptoms.

# Chapter 3

# Premarital and Marital Counseling

*The Sooner, the Better*

It has been my experience that marital problems top the list where people wait too long to call a therapist. Reaching out for marital counseling too late to try to salvage a "sinking ship" is, in many cases, the point of no return. Couples languish for years or even decades in unhappy marriages in which they put on a facade in public but cannot even look each other in the eye behind closed doors. Many couples stay married "for the kids," which would be great if only they were working on their relationship with the same logic. But before we look at when married couples should call a therapist, let's look at the premarital relationship, which is often fraught with problems the couple does not see or does not want to see right from the beginning. Please note that all names in the stories I share throughout the book have been changed to protect the privacy of those mentioned.

### Making a Tough Decision for an Upcoming Wedding

A woman came into my office one day and said in a straightforward way that she needed some professional feedback regarding her upcoming wedding. Susan outlined how she'd met her husband-to-be two years prior. She assessed their relationship as being very good. They reportedly had a lot in common, did many fun things together, and proclaimed their love to one another on a regular basis. The client added that they both shared the same outlook on the future, which included buying a house and having children. All seemed well for the couple until Susan revealed that her fiancé had been abusing his opioid pain medication. The client talked about how he had been out of work due to an injury on the job, had moved in with her because of financial issues, and had promised to help take care of her children while she was at work. However, she told me, he had been taking more prescription pain pills than he should. Susan went on to report how her fiancé would get agitated when he was out of his meds, and she noticed that he had been "doc shopping" during the day as a way to get prescriptions from as many sources as possible. She concluded by stating that his drug use had escalated to the point where one day she found a syringe in the bathroom, which made her fearful that her kids would find it and get injured.

Susan's question was "I love my fiancé, but I'm not so sure I should marry him. What should I do?" (See "What Is Your Definition of Love?" below) My first response was to restate what she had reported to see if I understood exactly what she was saying. I then asked, "What do your friends and family think you should do?" This is a question I often ask clients to get a feel for what the people close to them are saying. Susan reported that they'd all told her she should not get married, at least not at this point in time, and to wait until her fiancé got well again and went back to work (the family did not know the extent of the drug use because my client hid that from everyone). So even though the friends and family did not know about Susan's fiancé's drug problem, they reportedly still saw and heard enough that it put doubts in their minds. I sat back in my chair, looked my client in the eye, and talked about the enormous struggles that lay ahead for the couple due to his addiction. I educated her about the disease of addiction, opioids, and the difficulty of someone addicted to prescription pain meds (and street drugs) to get and remain sober. She began to cry. Part of me felt my client was hoping to hear that everything was going to be all right and that she should proceed with her marriage. And part of me felt she already knew the answer and was looking for a professional conformation. I asked my client what her tears were saying, and she talked about the investment of time, energy, and emotion she had put into the relationship and into helping her dreams come true. She no longer wanted to live as a single mom and thought she had found the person she could settle down with. Now she felt stuck and confused. At the end of the session, she thanked me for my frankness and honesty. She indicated that the session was helpful and that it gave her a lot to think about. Susan did not want to make a second appointment, but I indicated that she could call me if she wanted to talk. I never heard from her after that. I have no idea if she went through with the wedding, postponed it, or left the relationship. I just hoped the session had helped open her eyes to what lay ahead if she went forward with the wedding.

**What Is Your Definition of Love?**

Are there any points on the following list that may be in conflict with your definition of love?

I love you even though you . . .

◉ Blame me for all our problems and take little or no responsibility.

◉ Blatantly lie to me.

◉ Call me names.

◉ Hurt me emotionally.

◉ Hurt me physically.

◉ Cheat on me.

◉ Tell me you'll change but don't.

◉ Drink and use drugs to excess.

◉ Refuse to communicate with me.

◉ Refuse to listen to me; walk away while I'm talking.

◉ Give me the silent treatment after an argument.

◉ Talk negatively about me to family and friends.

◎ Spend money recklessly or lie about paying the bills.

◎ Work late every night even though you don't have to.

◎ Continually break promises.

◎ Have secret phone, text, and internet conversations.

◎ Constantly make excuses for your bad behavior

◎ Demonstrate anger by breaking, throwing, or punching things.

◎ Repeatedly threaten divorce or breakup.

◎ Use the kids as pawns in relationship problems.

◎ Don't like my family or friends.

◎ Blame your "traumatic" upbringing to justify current behaviors.

◎ Demand sex whenever you want it or withhold sex as punishment.

◎ Break the law with little or no concern for the consequences.

◎ Disregard special occasions such as birthdays and anniversaries.

◎ Hide important aspects of your life (prior marriages, children, prison, etc.).

◎ Refuse to seek help for obvious emotional, physical, or substance-abuse issues.

As you can see, the word *love* is often used out of context. It is true that people can love those who bring them pain, but I often ask my clients to gauge where their tolerance level is regarding hurtful behaviors. Some can tolerate a great deal of pain, others not so much. Everyone is different, and it is certainly heartbreaking to come to the realization that a spouse or significant other doesn't respect you or your feelings. This list is designed to bring awareness to not only your capacity to love but your spouse's or significant other's ability to love you. Mature love is the exact opposite of all the above statements. I believe that when clients say they love someone, it's important to ascertain whether it's mature love or just infatuation, passion, fear of being alone, denial, enabling, or codependence.

*Adjustments Needed When Living Together—Joe and Sarah*

Joe and Sarah dated for many years before getting married and had lived in separate residences when single. The two shared with me that they'd met through a mutual friend and had hit it off right from the beginning. Everyone thought they were going to get married right away, but they decided to wait until Joe finished his master's degree and they had saved some money. After four years, they tied the knot, and Joe moved into Sarah's apartment. The couple felt that the timing was right and figured that with their two incomes, they would be able to save money. It all seemed to make sense—waiting before getting married, Joe finishing school, and now saving money, post marriage, that they could put toward a house of their own. However, shortly after the couple married and moved in together, something started to change. They began to argue on a regular basis, something Joe said they had never done before. They were getting on each other's nerves, said they felt "trapped" in the apartment together, and were having problems distinguishing between whose money was whose and who should pay for what. When they were single and living in separate apartments, their money was their own and they could easily keep track of it as they budgeted for rent, utilities, and groceries. However, with their money combined and Joe making more money than Sarah, problems developed concerning where and how the money should be spent. In addition, Joe reported that he had never known how much time Sarah spent talking to her mother on the phone each day. When they were living separately, Joe was not there to see how much time Sarah was on the phone, but now this was something that began to annoy Joe as he felt that Sarah's mother was intrusive and taking too much of Sarah's time. More arguing ensued. Sarah had issues with Joe as well. She did not realize he went with friends after work for drinks a couple times a week. When single, the couple would talk on the phone later in the evening, and there was no mention as to what time Joe came home. Sarah complained about Joe's regular after-work drinks, which she thought were too frequent, and about the money he was spending at the bar, which could be better spent elsewhere.

A year passed, and the couple's problems grew more serious. Could this be the same couple who had been so happy for five years? Shortly thereafter, Joe decided to move out and get his own place. They equitably split the furniture they had purchased together and agreed to divide the money fairly. Finally, after time had passed with both Joe and Sarah on their own, they decided to divorce.

Four years dating each other and what they thought would be a lifetime of happiness had ended a little more than a year later. What happened? The couple and their relationship appeared to be in good shape the four years prior to getting married but fell apart shortly after they tied the knot. It appears they both did not factor the impact of living together on a day-to-day basis. Both were highly independent people and were able to manage very well on their own. They even managed to spend weekends at each other's apartments without any problems, but right after they moved in together, their single habits could not be merged in a seamless way. They both wanted to live as they'd lived before without the compromises and sacrifices they would have to make in order to live in harmony. As a dating couple living apart, they'd managed the kind of relationship that suited them both, where their individual habits and lifestyles did not impinge on one another. Getting married and moving in together made both Joe and Sarah feel trapped, which was something neither could deal with.

I saw Joe in individual therapy after he and Sarah had split up. It made me wonder what would have happened if the couple had sought marriage counseling early on in their marriage when their problems had just started to manifest. Joe reported that he and Sarah were too busy arguing to think about counseling, but he also indicated that it may have helped them work through their issues before they'd gotten out of hand. He said that their inability to mesh as a married couple brought about deep resentment and mistrust, and they'd reached a point where both just wanted out. Here is an example of a couple who appeared to be truly in love with one another as demonstrated by their four-year dating relationship. But after getting married and moving in together, it seems they were not prepared for the changes—having to share time, their living environment, and money in a way they never had to before. When the couple's problems started was the time to call a therapist who could help them understand their new realty and have a better chance of remaining married.

### "Love" Should Not Be a Battlefield—Eva and Mark

When Eva and Mark, a middle-class couple who had been married nineteen years, called me to come in for marriage counseling, I had no idea what I would see in the sessions. Their marriage was nothing short of a battleground and had been for many years. After the paperwork was completed and I asked how I could help them, both started talking at breakneck speed about all the injustices the other had inflicted upon them. Back and forth they went, like a tennis match, the accusations flying. Their marriage had been "bad" for a long time, and they'd decided to give it a last-ditch effort by coming to therapy. Therapy is sometimes used by married couples as a last stop before calling it quits. Is this the optimum time to call a therapist? Not even close. They should have started the process many, many years ago.

The couple described what had transpired in their marriage for years. Shouting matches with repetitive themes, accusations, name-calling, mistrust, and even physical altercations plagued their relationship on a regular basis. During one session, Mark related an incredible account of how Eva had actually ripped a door off the kitchen cabinets and thrown it at him. Eva reportedly proclaimed, "Well, if you didn't yell at me, I wouldn't have done it." I discussed the incident with the couple and the escalation they reported in their fighting and the implications if they continued. I was firm when I advised them that this kind of fighting had to stop *immediately*. Eva and Mark seemed to realize that their arguing had gotten out of control, but they continued to blame each other for their fights. Subsequent sessions consisted of repetitive arguing, with each trying to talk over the other and blaming them for what their marriage had become.

In my work, I explain to clients that I can help guide them, offer suggestions, and discuss options, but I cannot tell them what to do. There are a few exceptions, such as child and elder abuse, discovering that someone has suicidal or homicidal ideation or a plan to harm themselves or others (these are reportable situations), or when it appears that someone's living or working environment is so chaotic and unhealthy that remaining there could be a danger to their overall health. But in the above situation, I asked the couple if they had con-sidered getting a divorce since their behavior in the session was only a brief "snapshot" of what was going on at home. The couple said they had thought about divorce but gave a litany of reasons why they could not. Yet even as I pointed out that their behavior was like a broken record and that something in their relationship had to change (the couple actually agreed that something needed to change), their behav-ior in the sessions only continued in the same old pattern. More dis-cussion about divorce ensued, but again, the couple still came in to blame and berate each other. After the third session, they cancelled the next meeting and I never saw them again. I'm not sure what direction their marriage took, but I can only guess that the fighting, bickering, and disparaging comments continued. Here is an example of how far gone a relationship can be when, over the years, problems pile up with-out any intervention. When should this couple have called a therapist? Probably ten years prior, when their living environment had started to become toxic. I can only imagine what their day-to-day lives were like all those years with so much disdain toward one another.

*The Maturation of a Loving Relationship—Rita and George*

This last vignette is one of hope, love, and change in the evolution of a marital relationship. Rita and George had been married for twenty years in what was a second marriage for each. Both had children from their first marriages, which presented a challenging issue in and of itself. But the couple seemed to have effectively navigated their chil-dren's problems, as well as their own, over the years.

I met with them several years ago when they felt the love they had for each other was waning. They were both close to retirement age and had plans for when they would end their long careers in their respective fields. This presented stress in the relationship as the couple wondered if they were retiring at the right time and if they could manage financially. In addition, both Rita and George were experiencing elder-care responsibilities as it got closer to making decisions about where their parents would live out their remaining days. Their children would often present with their own issues, and it seemed there was way too much stress they were dealing with at the same time. Over the course of their marriage, the couple would talk freely about how they were feeling and would take turns listening and communicating with one another. They had decided at the beginning of their marriage that they would not repeat the same mistakes that had plagued their first marriages. They kept their marriage healthy by being thoughtful toward each other, they kept their intimacy alive, which they reportedly both enjoyed, and they maintained the most sacred element in any relationship—unconditional trust in each other. It wasn't until life "hit" all at once and from many different directions that they decided to come to therapy.

It was refreshing to see such a healthy couple in therapy. As mentioned earlier, many couples wait until they have run out of options before they decide to call a therapist, hoping that a "magic wand" can be waved to solve their problems. But this couple was different. They practiced love, respect, communication, listening skills, and had a healthy intimacy, which made them see one another as best friends. It wasn't rocket science to the couple; it was just loving and accepting each other for who they were. When they noticed that some of the glue that had kept their marriage together was starting to come apart, they reached out for help.

Subsequent sessions were used to discuss the trying time they were going through with multiple stressors coming at them all at once. We reviewed how they had maneuvered through problems in the past, and it was suggested that those same skills be used now. The couple acknowledged, and it was clear, that they loved each other very much. In the sessions, they became reacquainted with their strengths, which they were happy to see they still possessed. This couple, despite their problems, will succeed due to the strong foundation they built right from the beginning. They got into therapy at the right time—not after their disagreements had pushed them further apart but when they needed support from an objective professional who could clearly see that the two were, indeed, best friends for life.

## Elephant in the Room

The vast majority of marital problems can be worked through if the couple calls a therapist *sooner than later*. If you agree that going to marriage counseling would be helpful but your spouse disagrees, someone is not paying attention, which can be a big part of the problem. If one sees problems building in the relationship but the other feels everything is okay, how can everything be okay? In many cases, the husband in the relationship will proclaim, "I don't have a problem with our marriage. If you do, go and work through your issues." It's pretty clear that a couple cannot do couples counseling with only one person in the session. The situation is very telling if one spouse is not aware (or chooses not to be aware) and cannot respect the wishes of the other to go to therapy. Many times, it is discovered that there has been an "elephant" in the room for years without anyone talking about it. It's sad when some people know there are problems in the relationship but choose to do nothing about it.

## Common Signs That a Marriage Is in Trouble

When a couple decides to get married, it is usually a happy time in their lives. After spending some time getting to know one another, a proposal for marriage is often the next step. Attractiveness, kindness, a strong work ethic, being able to work through differences, and agreeing on having a family of their own are just a few of the values people base their decision to marry upon. A new marriage is filled with excitement and with the hope that dreams will become reality. So what happens when a marriage begins to fail? Below is a list of warning signs that a marriage is in trouble and that action should be taken sooner than later.

◉ The couple begins to bicker often over the same topics

◉ The arguments escalate out of control or become screaming matches

◉ The fighting often occurs in front of the kids

◉ One or both spouses start to detach emotionally

◉ The couple no longer enjoys spending time together

◉ Problem aren't discussed and are left unsettled

◉ Respect for one another begins to fade

◉ The level of intimacy is low, or there isn't any at all

◉ One spouse may become suspicious of the other upon finding "secrets"

◉ There is noticeable stress in the relationship that is making one or both spouses anxious and/or depressed

◉ A spouse is in frequent contact with old boyfriends or girl-friends on social media

◉ A couple may start arguing about where money is spent

◉ One spouse is happier when the other spouse is away from home

◉ There is the discovery that a spouse is making disparaging comments about the other to family or friends

◉ A spouse begins to cheat on the other emotionally and/or physically

◉ Alcohol and/or substance abuse begins or escalates

This list, although extensive, is not comprehensive, and there are numerous reasons a marriage will begin to unravel. The point here is to not wait until the marriage is beyond repair. Getting into therapy when problems first develop gives the marriage a better chance of survival than waiting until all the trust, respect, and love have disappeared.

## Divorce Statistics

Although it is difficult to ascertain (due to the many different measuring instruments and to irregular reporting), the actual percentages regarding divorce can be misleading. Some studies have calculated the current divorce rate to be 35 percent for millennials who wait until later to get married (assumedly they are more mature and have established careers) and 50 percent for those who married at an earlier age. Most studies report the divorce rate to be between 40 and 50 percent, with an average marriage length of eight years. Second marriages have a higher rate of divorce at 67 percent, and third marriages fail at a rate of 73 percent. Studies have attributed the high rate of second or more divorces to:

- ◉ People rushing to get married again or marrying on the "rebound"
- ◉ People not wanting to live a singles life
- ◉ People repeating the same mistakes they made in their previous marriage
- ◉ Individuals reading the "wrong signs" and being too quick to get out of a marriage they believe won't survive
- ◉ Blended-family problems
- ◉ Less "glue," or support systems, later in life

Getting into therapy after a divorce is not only wise for reasons of self-care, but it's also prudent to take a good, honest look at the marriage to see when and why it may have started to break down. Many partners will cast blame on their spouse and take little, if any, responsibility for their part in the breakup. It's difficult for them to look at their own flaws and admit their role in the failed marriage. But doing so can bring an awareness to negative, repetitious behavior and may help sustain their next marriage.

## Marital "Tune-Up"

In my work with couples over the years, I've found that the only way to stave off marital problems before they fester is to *call a therapist before the problems become too big to change.* I like to think of it in terms of maintaining a car. Most people bring their car to the shop on a regular basis. Diagnostics are performed, the oil gets changed, the tires are rotated, and other maintenance is performed in order to keep the car in good working order. Without this periodic preventative maintenance, problems that are more costly to repair than a simple tune-up can develop. What about a marriage? Why don't people take the same approach with their relationship as they do with their automobiles? When an issue comes up with our car, most of us bring it to the shop so that the problem doesn't get worse. Why isn't the same concept used with problems in the marriage? Years ago when I was much younger, I owned a Chevy van I bought primarily to go camping in the summer in New England. It was a good purchase because it carried a lot and could be used for sleeping if the weather was too bad to pitch a tent. It was very versatile even when it wasn't used for camping. Years later, I made the mistake of not keeping up with the oil maintenance, and initially a little smoke began to come out the back, which was the first sign that something was wrong. I ignored the problem, and more and more smoke began to come out, which later resulted in damage to the piston rings, valves, and other engine parts, which ultimately rendered the motor inoperative. I ended up selling it to a mechanic who planned to replace the entire engine because the motor could not be fixed. The moral of the story? Please call a therapist when you see a small amount of "smoke." Do not wait until the marriage is so bad it requires a complete "overhaul," which may not even be possible. In the long run, these periodic relationship tune-ups will keep things running smoothly for years to come.

I would like to end this chapter by adding one more important point for all married couples to consider. Often, when problems develop in a marriage, one or both spouses will complain to friends, colleagues, or family members about what they are going through. Each spouse will describe their troubles from their individual perspective which, in all likelihood, is skewed to some extent. Each spouse is looking for not only comfort and support but also validation and a sense that they are the one being victimized. Sides are taken, the couple gets "advice" from others who want to be there for them, and a spouse hears morphed information they take as fact. The situation now grows from a bump in the marital road to a battleground between his-and-her camps. Each spouse hears a litany of what they should or should not do, which can exacerbate the couple's problems.

My advice to a couple going through a "rough patch" is to keep their problems to themselves and to get into therapy to work through their issues. Labeling and demonizing the respective spouse is like putting a wedge between the couple from which the marriage may never recover. Harsh words will be spoken, people will be blamed, and situations not even related to the couple's issues will come up, thus effectively pouring gasoline onto the fire. I believe a marriage is a sacred place that should only be occupied by two. If anyone else tries to enter that place, one person must leave. Keep your marriage intact and don't let anyone else in. The thought here is if the disagreement can be worked through, the relationship will be a much stronger union and the couple can move forward and learn from their issues. If the whole world gets involved, accusations, finger-pointing, and irrelevant advice will fly, and a relatively small matter can turn into irreconcilable situation.

---

The only exception to bringing other people into the problems in a marriage is if there is abuse, of any nature and toward anyone, in the home. This kind of behavior is not okay under any circumstance. Safety and support are what is needed immediately so that the abused person can get help as soon as possible. This topic is discussed further in chapter 12, "Abuse and Neglect."

---

Chapter 4

# Anxiety
## *Your Shrinking World*

A nxiety can be a mild nervous feeling that can actually give us energy, sharpen our thinking, and allow us to move out of our comfort zones to try something different, or it can produce fear and worry, sap our energy, and cause us to withdraw from life. At lower levels, anxiety and excitement can closely resemble one another. Think of getting a promotion, skydiving, buying a home for the first time, or getting married. All four examples can be anxiety-producing and exciting at the same time. However, there is a different kind of anxiety that can go far beyond excitement and send people into a state of panic. This is where catastrophic or negative thinking can bring about unrelenting fear. It is the kind of anxiety that can paralyze a person and shrink one's world into a prison without walls. When is the time to call a therapist? Let's first take a look at the problems that can arise from living in the past and worrying about the future. We will then look at specific anxiety disorders; what their presentation looks like, including symptoms and behaviors; and when to take action and call a therapist, which, as always, should be sooner than later.

## Stuck in the Past/Fearing the Future

When I encounter clients who talk about their anxiety, I find many are either dwelling in the past or trying to predict the future. A lot of people continue to worry about something they said or did, or something a loved one said or did, many years after the situation has passed. They may be stuck in the past and continue to bring up old marital issues, problematic family-of-origin situations, or any other issue they cannot or will not let go of. These folks cannot move forward. They often play the role of victim and martyr. Here are a few examples of someone living in the past:

- ◉ I still cannot get over what you said to my sister last Thanksgiving.
- ◉ I should have known better when I first married you.
- ◉ Are you going to lose this job, too?
- ◉ You remind me of your mother when you do that.
- ◉ I have to keep my eye on you at all times so that you don't relapse.

Others engage in future worry called the "what-if's":

- ◉ What if I go to the party and see my ex? We have a lot of friends in common.
- ◉ What if I go out to my car and my tire is flat? What will I do?
- ◉ I'm taking my exam next week. What if I don't pass it?
- ◉ What if it rains on the day of our family barbeque?
- ◉ What if my mother doesn't like what I am wearing?

As you can see, we can what-if anything. These folks are trying to predict the future. The negative event hasn't even happened yet, but people think, "Yeah, but *what if* it does?" For the record, we can counter that question with another question, "But what if it *doesn't* happen?" Makes sense, but there is no stopping people who really want to worry. What people often fail to recognize is if something not in their plans occurs, they, as adults, have the capacity to figure out what to do. We are capable of dealing with any of the scenarios mentioned above and the many other situations that may come up in our lives. Yes, having to change a flat tire is not something anyone wants to do, especially after a long workday, but if it does occur, we have the capacity to deal with it one way or another. We need to trust that we can handle whatever comes our way, whether by ourselves or with the help of others, and know that whatever we encounter will not remain that way for long.

## Worrying for Nothing

No one has a "crystal ball" to the future. Anything can happen, and sometimes things just do not go our way. Using the example of the flat tire, 99.9 percent of the time we go to our car, start the engine, and drive away without a second thought. If we worried all day about leaving work only to find a flat tire, we would have worried eight hours of our day for absolutely nothing. Who wants to do that? I don't.

Now, in that rare .1 percent of the time when we leave work and we do have a flat tire, what do we do? Pronounce that it must be the end of the world and sit in the parking lot and cry? Blame the automobile manufacturer and swear you'll never buy another one of "those" cars again? Kick the tire until you hurt your foot? That's not going to get your tire fixed. Fortunately, as adults, we can come up with several solutions to the problem. Some may be more palatable than others depending on the circumstances you find yourself in. Here are some solutions:

◉ You can change the tire yourself.

◉ If the tire is not entirely flat, you can drive to a service station.

◉ Call A A A if you have that service.

◉ Call a friend or relative for help.

◉ Ask a coworker to assist you.

◉ Take a taxi or Uber home and get it fixed the next day.

Those are six solutions, and there may be more, to deal with that .1-percent-of-the-time annoyance no one likes. It simply isn't worth worrying about the possibility of this rare event for the entire day on the off chance it may happen when we've seen that chances are it won't.

It is not worth the energy and time, not to mention that gut-wrenching feeling that comes with worrying all day long for nothing. We can't predict the future, but worrying about something that hasn't happened yet is counterproductive.

Here's another example of trying to predict the future: "What if I don't pass my licensing exam?" Many people worry like this before an important test of any kind. Although it may be a common occurrence, it does no good to think negative thoughts about your performance days or even hours before the exam. I know people who worried so much about not passing an exam that the built-up anxiety turned out to be the reason they did not get a passing score. Their worry became a self-fulfilling prophecy.

Many people have the knowledge base to pass exams, but in some cases, the anxiety prevents that knowledge from being accessed. Any ability to think and recall effectively is used up by focusing on the anxiety. Below are a few tips to consider prior to taking an exam:

- ◉ Give yourself sufficient time to review any preparatory material.
- ◉ Take a class on sample questions that may be on the exam.
- ◉ Use exercise to help lower anxiety.
- ◉ Get proper rest the day and night before the test.
- ◉ Have something to eat and drink the day of the exam.
- ◉ Go into the test with a positive mindset.
- ◉ Talk to others who have passed the test.
- ◉ Know that more than likely, you can retake the test if necessary.

As mentioned earlier, a little bit of anxiety can energize us and sharpen our minds, but a lot of anxiety can actually do the opposite. Practice how to gauge where your anxiety level is, like biofeedback, sometime before the exam to try to decide which coping strategies will help lower the stress.

## Living in the Present—Where Reality Resides

In my practice, I use the technique of mindfulness I learned in an intensive dialectical behavioral therapy (DBT) course I took in Seattle. Mindfulness is focusing on the here and now, the present, without going to the past (which we cannot change) or into the future (something that isn't here yet). The only real time we have is in the present moment. This is where we experience life—not in the past or in the future but right here, right at this very moment.

Mindfulness exercises consist of using just about any object you can find. A piece of paper, a pen, or even raisins can be used, to name a few things. The idea is to engage your sense of sight, sound, touch, smell, and, if practical, taste, in the exercise. If you are working with a small box of raisins, you may use all your senses to explore them:

*Look* at the color, shape, and size of the raisins in the box.

*Listen* for any sound as you shake the box.

*Touch* them; pour some raisins into the palm of your hand and feel the softness.

*Smell* the raisins in your hand.

*Taste* the raisins and feel the texture with your tongue.

A mindfulness session may take only ten minutes and then we talk about the experience. I ask my client how he/she felt during and after the exercise. We discuss the process, and I ask if the client was able to focus only on the raisins for the entire ten minutes. If my client could focus the entire time, we talk about what it was like to be in the present moment for the full amount of time. If not, we look at what may have been a distraction. The purpose of a mindfulness exercise is to be so engaged in the present using all of our senses that the past and future cannot impinge on the experience. I remind my clients that the past is gone and cannot be changed and the future is not here yet. The only real time we have is the present. When someone continues to go back to the past or venture into the future, I have them do a mindfulness exercise to help bring them into the present. Mindfulness can be practiced at home or the office, while walking or doing dishes, or during medita‑ tion. As long as you can be present in what you are doing, it helps you to remain "real" to what's happening in the here and now. Interestingly, some people do not like being in the here and now. Reality can be too intense and one's problems too overwhelming. In their mind, they may go back in time to when there were fewer issues to cope with, or they may fantasize about a better future. Some people escape through all types of activities and addictions in order to soothe the pain and anxi‑ ety of reality. Reality is not always easy, but to run away from it by living in the past or future can delay better times and even make folks lose a sense of who they are. If we avoid working through our issues in the here and now, we are like ghosts of the past and future, which can be more painful than the actual anxiety one is trying to escape. Let's look at some specific anxiety disorders and discuss when it would be time to call a therapist for help.

### Generalized Anxiety Disorder (GAD)

Generalized anxiety disorder (GAD) is a condition of feeling anxious all the time. The anxiety is "generalized" because it can be driven by a number of circumstances in our lives. Financial, work, relationship, marriage, health, and family issues are just some of the areas that can generate this kind of anxiety. Often, anxiety is multifaceted in that it can come from several areas at the same time.

The centerpiece of generalized anxiety disorder is worry, and those suffering from this disorder worry about everything. Some dwell about the past or incessantly worry about the future. And in most instances, the amount of worrying is out of proportion to the actual likelihood of the feared events happening.

Generalized anxiety disorder, which may have developed when we were younger, can carry on right through adulthood. Negative thinking, excessive worry, fear of the unknown, constant restlessness, difficulty concentrating, irritability, somatic issues, and poor sleep are some of the symptoms of GAD. This condition negatively affects relationships, jobs and possible promotions, friendships, and even our health in general. It is like constantly being "on" and waiting for something bad to happen, which almost always doesn't happen.

The parents of children and teens need to recognize that there is a problem and then take corrective measures. If that doesn't happen, disorders like GAD won't just go away, they will linger and make the person's life very uncomfortable. Many sufferers actually believe this is the way life is supposed to be and that everyone feels the same way. Until the person realizes that not everyone is suffering like they are, they are unlikely to do something about it. The earlier a therapist is consulted for treatment, the sooner life will become less uncomfortable, less dangerous, less frightening, and less worrisome.

Like many anxiety disorders, the causes of GAD are not fully known. And like other disorders, it may be a combination of heredity, past childhood experiences, and the environment. Psychologists Aaron Beck and Gary Emery believe generalized anxiety disorder is sustained by "basic fears," such as fear of losing control, fear of not being able to cope, fear of failure, fear of rejection or abandonment, or fear of disease or death.[1] For the purposes of this book, we will not go much deeper into the theoretical aspects of GAD but focus more on how the presentation of the disorder and the symptoms of GAD can affect one's life.

Having generalized anxiety disorder is a scary way to go through life. I know because I suffered from GAD when I was younger. It seemed like everything and everyone was reason to worry and fear. I was in constant tension that at any given moment something bad was going to happen. And the not knowing from where or from whom or when doom would strike only perpetuated the anxiety. I thought that if I felt like something bad was going to happen, something bad would happen. Generalized anxiety disorder is like waiting for something bad to happen all the time. It's being hypervigilant all the time, like a soldier in war on the lookout for the enemy. It's important to note that just because we think or feel like something bad is going to occur, it doesn't mean it's actually going to happen. Our central nervous system can actually be "tricked" into believing this way. Small problems in our lives can be built to disproportional or catastrophic heights. Why? As mentioned above, it may be due to our upbringing in the home, our genetic makeup, learned behavior, or other reasons. It may not be all that important to know the "why" of anxiety. It is the treatment that will produce the best results in the here and now.

## My Personal Experience with GAD

I do not remember having generalized anxiety disorder when I was very young. I played, went to school, and had what I thought was a normal home life. It wasn't until my parents and I moved out of the city and into the suburbs that I remember my anxiety beginning to escalate. I remember having to make new friends in my neighborhood and at school, acclimate to a new town, and live a new lifestyle, all the while being resistant to the changes. I had left everything I knew back in the old neighborhood—friends, school, neighbors, and the city where I was born. Transitioning to suburban life proved a bit of a culture shock. I felt "different" in the suburbs. My city mentality did not mesh well with the suburban kids. Being the new kid in school, I endured some mild bullying until I made friends who are still in my life to this day. But the feeling that I was walking on eggshells persisted from the time of the move, through my teen years, and well into my twenties.

Later, high school proved boring, and my grades reflected it. I didn't care. I was spinning in my own anxiety, and I didn't know how to get off the merry-go-round. This would have been the time to call a therapist, but as a kid, what did I know about therapy and therapists? My father had a blue-collar job, and my mother was a housewife. They did not know about therapy, and even if they did, it was unlikely they would pay to talk to someone when they thought all you had to do was "snap out of it." It wouldn't be until years later when I was on my own that I sought help and began to sort through my issues.

When we are young, we have to rely on our parents to make the call to a therapist. Many believe their kids will grow out of it or it's just a phase they're in. However, times have changed, and parents are better educated and attuned to their children's performance and behavior in and out of school. An astute parent will recognize problems with their child, and if talking to their kids at home or in parent-teacher meetings does not help, they know it's time to call a child or adolescent therapist—someone who works specifically with this population.

## Obsessive Compulsive Disorder (OCD)

Obsessive-compulsive disorder (OCD) is often a catchphrase for people who see themselves as overly tidy or as someone who is a stickler for details at work or at home. A little OCD may not be a bad thing and may actually help people be more organized. However, as one goes up the continuum, obsessive-compulsive disorder can shrink a person's world to the extent that most or all their time is spent on routines and rituals practiced in isolation.

Obsessions can be recurring thoughts, ideas, images, or impulses that seem senseless and can be intrusive in one's mind. Examples may include fears of leaving the stove on or doors unlocked at home, to images of violence or thoughts of doing violence or harm to a loved one. Although these thoughts can be looked at as irrational, they continue to invade one's mind for hours, days, and sometimes even years. In many cases, these thoughts are unrelated to real-life problems.

Compulsions are behaviors or rituals performed to expel the anxiety caused by obsessions. Examples include washing hands numerous times to counter a fear of being contaminated, constantly checking the doors or stove, or having a "system" of marking items in the home to be able to see if they have been moved. Many people realize that these rituals are unreasonable yet feel compelled to do them as a way to ward off the anxiety associated with a particular obsession. The conflict between the wish to be free of the compulsive rituals and the irresistible desire to perform them is a great source of anxiety.

In addition to those mentioned above, common compulsions include taking numerous, long showers every day; washing, vacuuming, and waxing one's car daily; and collecting anything and everything, more commonly known as hoarding.

The key to anxiety disorders, including obsessive-compulsive disorder, is what many call "runaway" catastrophic thinking and erroneous belief systems. If we learn early on, for example, that getting too close to other people can be dangerous, we form a belief system based on what we are told, especially if it is repeated verbally as well as demonstrated to us. We all know that not everyone is a person to avoid and that the vast majority of people are decent human beings. And we know as adults that there are certain places, people, and situations we're better off avoiding. But where is the line drawn? Most people will trust first, and then if a problem develops, will reassess the situation and move in what they believe is a less risky direction.

Not so with people who have OCD. Due to their false belief system that everyone is potentially dangerous and should be avoided, they may reason that getting close to others is risky and that there are only a few people who can be trusted, such as close friends or relatives. It's an internal system that is in reverse of the way most people think and can be perpetuated by as little as a story on the six o'clock news about someone being robbed. An erroneous belief system coupled with runaway what-if thinking can take a benign event and turn it into a nightmare.

Someone with catastrophic thinking may say, "I don't want to go to New York City because I was told people get mugged there." I may ask, "Where did you get that thought from?" The person may answer, "My parents told me to never go into the City because of the high crime rate there." Here is where logic in a situation like this fails. New York City is a big city, like many other big cities, and the crime rate is probably higher due to the greater population of people who live there, but statistically, crime has actually dropped over the years. Not everyone gets robbed in New York City. This is where the what-ifs come in. "Yeah, but what if we're in the subway and someone pulls a gun?" or

"What if a gang of kids tries to steal my wallet?" or "What if a crazy cab driver swerves and hits us?" As you can see, an erroneous belief system, together with runaway thinking, can lead to numerous scenarios that in all probability will never happen. The problem is that any one of these events *could* possibly happen, but the odds are very, very small.

When I am feeling playful, I'll say to my client that if they are so sure a terrible event is going to happen to them and they can predict it in advance, maybe they should select the winning lottery numbers so they can retire to a life of leisure. When they tell me they cannot do that, I question it because it appears that if they can predict terrible things will happen in the future, why not something good like the winning lottery?

### Escalation in Negative Thinking

Another issue with obsessive-compulsive disorder is that as time goes by, one obsession can lead to more obsessions, ranging from someone checking the stove ten times to believing they have a terrible disease and will die despite numerous medical professionals stating they are fine and have a clean bill of health. One erroneous obsession can lead to other erroneous beliefs, which compounds the problem. As I tell many of my clients, the longer they wait to begin the work of challenging and changing their old belief systems, the more their world will continue to shrink to the point where they do not feel safe outside their own home. Cognitive-behavioral therapy (CBT) and dialectical-behavioral therapy (DBT) can help change erroneous thought patterns and compulsive behaviors, and other behavior-modification strategies, such as exposure-and-response prevention, can also be helpful. Medication from a psychiatrist is another helpful route one can pursue for mediating OCD.

### Signs It's Time to Call a Therapist

So, when should someone call a therapist if one's thoughts and behaviors are interfering with life? As early as possible! If the child, adolescent, or young adult is living in a functional home, parents or caregivers can look for the signs and symptoms of OCD, which may manifest outside the home or at school. Obsessive-compulsive disorder sufferers may need their homework to be "perfect" or may spend an inordinate amount of time studying for an exam or working and reworking a project, sometimes to the point the project doesn't get completed. They may wash their clothes excessively or not wear clothes they feel are "contaminated." At school they may get picked on when other kids find that they can get a strong reaction from someone who doesn't like their belongings touched. Or a teacher may pick up on a message in an essay that indicates that if the child thinks they are not good enough, something bad may happen to someone close to them. This would be the time for a parent to call a therapist to discuss why these behaviors may be happening and how to address them as soon as possible. However, if the child or adolescent is living in a dysfunctional home where irrational beliefs are the norm, a person may struggle with their OCD for some time before they get help. Sometimes sufferers need to take note from others around them. A teacher, friend, another family member, or a college roommate may begin to point out odd patterns of behavior, and if tuned in enough to the person in need, they will see that the individual requires help. As a person gets older, their symptoms may manifest in more obvious ways. At a time when most people's worlds should be opening up (doing things with friends, driving, beginning college, dating, starting a career), for someone with OCD, the world shrinks as they isolate more and more. These are signs that something is wrong and that they or someone close to them should call a therapist. Here, the process of untangling all the false beliefs can begin so the individual learns that their world is far less dangerous then they believe it to be.

### Panic Disorder and Anxiety Attacks

Panic disorder and anxiety attacks are intense episodes of fear that seem to come out of the blue for no apparent reason. These "attacks" may last only a few minutes, but for sufferers, they can seem like an eternity. During a panic attack, a person may think they are having a heart attack or stroke. Some have reported feeling like they are going crazy. These thoughts may actually escalate the intensity, producing a downward spiral of panic. After repeated episodes, a person may visit an array of doctors, believing that they must have a cardiac condition, pulmonary issue, or even a brain tumor. Sufferers will often see numerous specialists, and with no medical problems found, they may get a recommendation to begin counseling. This is the time to call a therapist, but many dealing with panic disorder will try to figure out their issues on their own. This often only prolongs the suffering. Recommendations to see a psychiatrist for antianxiety medication may also be met with resistance, with patients proclaiming, "I don't take pills to solve my problems."

Some of the symptoms experienced during a panic attack are:

- ⊚ Heart palpitations/pounding heart
- ⊚ Dizziness
- ⊚ Shortness of breath or shallow breathing
- ⊚ Trembling or shaking
- ⊚ Sweating
- ⊚ Abdominal distress
- ⊚ Feeling "out of it," or not connected to reality
- ⊚ Tingling in hands or feet
- ⊚ Cold sweats
- ⊚ Tightness in chest
- ⊚ Fear of losing control
- ⊚ Fear of dying

Not all of the above will be experienced during an anxiety attack. Though an attack may consist of a limited number of symptoms, the episode can feel like multiple physical and emotional processes are affected simultaneously.

## Downward Spiral

A secondary problem with panic disorder is the worry associated with having another panic attack. This underlying worry may actually predispose someone to having another attack, and a cycle of worry and panic develops. This may also cause someone to be hypervigilant or to develop anticipatory anxiety, where the person is just waiting for the beginnings of another panic attack. This fear of the fear can be confusing to a sufferer as they find that it is not only the panic they worry about but the associated anxiety surrounding the panic.

Anxiety, panic, and excessive worry can shrink a person's world until they find they are doing less and less of the activities they once enjoyed. They may decide to not go out into the "dangerous" world because they fear the unknown. This may lead to another complication called agoraphobia. Agoraphobia is essentially the fear of having a panic attack in places where escape is difficult. Sufferers may start avoiding places where they believe help cannot get to them in time if they begin to panic or that they may embarrass themselves by acting "crazy" in a crowd.

Anxiety can build on top of anxiety, and the longer one waits to call a therapist, the longer it can take to remove the layers of anxiety. Hopefully, one will call a therapist early on, when anxiety attacks are just beginning, rather than watch as complications develop.

In my practice, I have noticed a number of situations where panic disorder has developed. In many cases, my clients have been going through some form of transition in their lives. Regardless of age or gender, major changes in one's life, even positive changes, can cause panic attacks that appear illogical to the untrained eye, but through the examples below, I hope to demonstrate how these types of transitions can lead to panic disorder.

## Transitions Can Cause Anxiety—Bill

I first met Bill after he received a degree in business from a prestigious university, landed an amazing job on Wall Street, and began suffering from panic disorder a few months after he began work. All aspects of Bill's life seemed to be on track for him to have a successful career in finance. He finished college with a 3.8 GPA and beat out a number of eligible candidates for his position. Bill reported no unusual issues in his personal life, and according to his family, Bill excelled at everything he put his mind to. What could possibly be going on in Bills life that had him worrying about going into work every morning?

I decided to explore Bill's life before he landed his dream job to see where his anxiety might be emanating from. Bill had lived in New Jersey all his life but a few days a week, he commuted to Fordham University in New York City. His commute took him from New Jersey and over the George Washington Bridge for classes and to go out with friends who lived in and around the City.

Bill reported that he had no recollection of ever having debilitating anxiety in his youth, in high school, or in college, but something had changed after he started working in New York. Bill started experiencing panic attacks that came without warning. Bill was also experiencing anxiety at work, which distracted him and also drew the attention of his boss. As time went on, he became hypervigilant and was always on guard. This obsessing about the panic seemed to exacerbate the problem as the panic attacks came more frequently and with greater intensity. Bill felt confused, lost, and scared about what was happening to the point where he seriously thought about leaving his job to look for work in New Jersey.

At the urging of his parents, Bill picked up the phone and called for help months after his anxiety began. He was perplexed as to why he was experiencing anxiety after all the hard work he'd put into receiving his degree and landing a great job.

I thought long and hard as to why Bill was experiencing panic now when he had previously traveled to New York and back without a second thought. The only thing I could put my finger on was that Bill had experienced a transition from having relatively few responsibilities as a college kid to college graduate and then an employee in a well-known company. It all began to make sense. Bill had no problem driving into the City to take classes or meet friends before graduating, but now that he had transitioned from having a little responsibility to having a lot, Bill developed an underlying fear that he would not be able to live up to his new role as an important employee in a big firm. Before, his only responsibility was to study and maintain his grades. Now he had tremendous responsibility in managing other people's assets. All of a sudden the carefree kid had responsibilities he'd never imagined. And it had happened so fast.

We determined that Bill had developed a panic disorder because he was unsure that he could perform up to his boss's expectations and he worried about producing for a company that had put their faith in him. That's a lot of pressure for someone to take on not too long after they considered themselves just a college bum. It was the sudden transition from having relatively few responsibilities to being thrust into the world of finance that scared Bill, which almost caused him to retreat and quit his job.

Bill and I worked on his self-esteem and value and talked about whether he deserved to be so successful at such a young age. We explored his academic career, and he came to be comfortable with knowing he had finished at the top of his class. And we realized that the bridge he had trouble crossing after college had become a symbol of this transition from a kid with nothing to worry about to an adult with responsibilities that were now an everyday occurrence.

While in therapy, Bill began to feel comfortable with this transition and began to excel at his job. In time, he was able to face his fears not only about being able to cross the bridge but to see himself as a valuable member of his company's team. Eventually, Bill's anxiety diminished to the point that he did not even think about it anymore. The transition had scared him, but after therapy, he began to understand what his anxiety was telling him. Would Bill have spared himself much anguish had he entered therapy earlier? In my opinion, yes, but the fact that he entered therapy at all is a testament to Bill's strength to get the bottom of his issues.

*Reinventing Himself—Mike*

At age fifty-four, Mike had worked for the government his entire adult life and had a job that awarded him high-level security clearance. Mike and his wife had four children and were kept busy with homework, school projects, sports, clubs, fund-raisers, and any activity that involved their children. They were a close family who vacationed in the summer, celebrated birthdays and the holidays with extended family, and were there to support one another when times were tough. Mike and his wife were pretty much on the same page when it came to decisions about their kids, and they were proud of their incredibly stable-minded children. When their older kids went off to college, Mike and his wife were kept busy with the younger ones who were finishing high school. They considered their marriage "good" as they navigated the vicissitudes of life side by side. Theirs was a typical modern-day family who enjoyed the fun times and handled the difficult times in measured ways.

Mike's job with the government began after he left the military. He was an intelligence specialist in the army and enjoyed the work. As time went by, he advanced within his government job and security clearance. Mike worked alongside brilliant men and women and with state-of-the-art equipment on important projects. After working hard for a number of years, he had become a valued member of the team. Mike eventually put in over thirty years and planned to start his own private security company after he retired.

Over time, all of Mike's children had either graduated from college and were out on their own or still in college. After being so busy dealing with all the ins and outs of raising children, Mike and his wife found themselves alone in their home for the first time in twenty-five years. At the same time, Mike retired from his government job and began to work toward opening his private security firm. Everything was starting to fall into place, but something strange was happening to Mike. He began having panic attacks that confused and upset him. He never remembered having anxiety attacks before. He admitted being anxious when he and his wife were married, bought their first house, and started having children. But he never remembered having anxiety at work, knowing he was well trained and a "rising star" in his career. Mike was perplexed as to why he was experiencing panic attacks at this point in his life.

So Mike did what nearly everyone does when panic sets in. He went from doctor to doctor to see if he had a medical condition that could explain what was happening. When every doctor he visited gave him a clean bill of health, Mike became unsure of himself. This should be a good time in his life, Mike thought, but now his confidence had become affected, and he became despondent. Shortly thereafter, he took the advice of one of his doctors and scheduled a therapy session with me.

To help Mike rebuild his confidence, I let him know I had worked with other clients who had the same symptoms he was experiencing and that he was not alone. I also shared my observations over the years regarding transitions, and I described what I saw occurring in his life. I pointed out how he'd been ambitious in his early years and seemed to know what type of career he wanted for himself. He'd worked hard, earned a government job he was proud of, married and had children, and had been busy with life until recently. Now it was like someone had put on the brakes and life had ground to a halt. The kids still needed Mike's help when they had issues, but the hustle and bustle of everyday life had changed remarkably. And the fact that Mike had left a position he knew well to open his own company only added to the unknown that lay ahead of him. And Mike's relationship with his wife had gone from a reportedly good place to where they mostly talked in generalities or about their children. Mike had assumed the next phase of his life would go as smoothly as the rest had gone, and he was surprised by the strength of the underlying anxiety precipitated by the transitions he was undergoing.

Mike and I examined all the changes that were occurring in his life at about the same time. Mike had many questions. "Am I still important to my children and my wife?" "Did I make the right decision to quit my job when I did?" "Will I succeed in my new role in my own company?" "When will I actually be able to retire?"

Once we discussed his track record with having the ability to get what he wanted in his life, Mike began to see his transitions as something not to fear but to conquer as he did with all the other obstacles in his life. He also began to realize that his kids would always need him and always see him as an anchor, someone they knew they could go to when they encountered their own struggles. Mike also realized that over the course of his marriage, his wife had always been there for him and had supported him throughout his career.

After many weeks of hard work in therapy, Mike began to see how the multiple, simultaneous transitions in his life had scared him, thus precipitating his anxiety attacks. His insight and understanding into his anxiety began to make sense to him. He started to realize that much he had feared was due to underlying processes that had begun to erode his confidence. This diminished confidence caused him to doubt not only his value but whether he had it in him to build a successful company at this stage in his life. Slowly and consistently, Mike became stronger, and his self-esteem began grew. He was now able to look at his life and see all he had accomplished, and he could envision the future he wanted to build for himself. Mike could now see that the major changes he'd experienced were all for the good and a natural part of progression in a healthy family.

Mike and his wife came into therapy for a few sessions and talked about where they were in their marriage and vowed to spend more time together. Concerning Mike's company, he reached out to a couple of former coworkers who were also retired and who agreed to work as consultants with Mike in putting together a security company. It wasn't long before they began to get contracts through their connections in the field.

When was the right time to call a therapist? Mike called for a session shortly after one of his doctors recommended he talk to a therapist. Mike did not prolong his agony or ignore his anxiety. Nor did

Mike let his ego get the better of him or talk himself out of going to therapy. Because Mike called a therapist at about the right time, he began to successfully move forward with his life.

*Multiple Role Changes—Rosemary*

Rosemary began having anxiety attacks after her husband became gravely ill. He had been in and out of hospitals after his heart attack, and when he was home, she nursed him around the clock. Rosemary was a nurse herself and, as such, was familiar with acute and chronic illnesses. She comforted him in every way possible and only got a break from caregiving when his health would decline and he would need hospitalization. After years of caring for her husband, she found herself alone one day when he passed away. Rosemary loved her husband but realized now that he was released from his suffering, she could move on with her life. Rosemary thought that all her anxiety was a result of caring for her husband, but after he died, her anxiety became more persistent.

She began to have increasing anxiety and anxiety attacks on a regular basis, and the phenomenon of "fearing the fear" started to take hold. Rosemary was now hypervigilant about having anxiety attacks, which led to more attacks.

She decided to take some time off work, hoping that getting away from the hospital where she worked would do her good. But on the very first day away from her hospital, she had an anxiety attack as she ran her routine errands around town. This bothered Rosemary so much she did not even want to go out of the house anymore.

Believing that going back to work would keep her distracted, Rosemary went back to her regular rotation, but her anxiety continued to escalate, and she was having anxiety attacks almost every day. Rosemary was confused as she began to confide in her friends about her issues and was given "advice" from just about all of them.

One of her friends suggested she get away for a while and offered her home in the Poconos as a place Rosemary could go to relax and unwind. Rosemary decided to take her up on the offer and thought it would do her good, so she packed a bag, got the directions, and proceeded to Pennsylvania. But as she approached a bridge that spanned the Delaware River, she experienced such strong anxiety that she had to pull off to the side of the road. Rosemary's heart was beating fast, and she was sweating and feeling so dizzy she did not believe she could continue to her destination. She wound up calling the friend who'd offered her home to explain what happened and, filled with embarrassment, asked her friend if she and another friend could come and get her and drive her home. Feeling defeated, Rosemary got home but did not leave the house for many days after that.

Rosemary's life was much the same for almost a year. Like many others in the same situation, she had gone to a number of specialists trying to get to the bottom of things. And like others, no medical condition could be found. Rosemary began to use compensatory measures to cope and avoid places that triggered the most anxiety.

Unfortunately, her job seemed to bring her the most stress, and she would find herself going into work late or calling out sick on a regular basis. Her attendance was noticed by her manager, and they had a meeting to address this issue. Rosemary's boss had all her paperwork in order and presented her with all her late punches and all the days she'd called out sick, which were usually Mondays and Fridays. When asked for an explanation, Rosemary opened up and talked about her husband dying a year earlier and her struggles with anxiety and anxiety attacks, her problems with leaving the house, and her growing isolative behaviors. After about a half-hour meeting, Rosemary's manager suggested she utilize the company's employee assistance program (EAP), which offered free therapy sessions for employees. Rosemary agreed to go.

At the time, I was working for the company that provided EAP services, and Rosemary became my client. She talked about the last three years of being her husband's caregiver and her issues with anxiety during that time and since he died. She also talked about how her anxiety was preventing her from driving even moderate distances, and she detailed the anxiety attack she experienced while on the trip to the Poconos. Rosemary appeared defeated.

I began my work with her in a systematic way where we looked at her life with her husband before his illness, during his illness, and after he died. Her anxiety showed a complexity that only a thorough examination could uncover. It appeared Rosemary's anxiety had been building for years as she'd transitioned from a good marriage with her husband, through his illness, and then to his death. At each phase, Rosemary's role changed—from wife to caregiver to widow. Interestingly, just after her husband's death, Rosemary was diagnosed with cardiac issues, which frightened her, especially since her husband had died from complications of a heart attack. Now Rosemary had developed a fear of dying, which only complicated her anxiety issues.

The first thing I focused on with Rosemary was mindfulness. Mindfulness is keeping our attention in the present moment, away from the past and not on the future. Many people increase their anxiety by dredging up the past, a place we have no longer have control over and cannot undo. As we worked on being mindful and in the moment, we discussed all the transitions she had gone through that coincidently matched her increasing anxiety over the years as well as the many roles she had played since her husband's heart attack. We also explored her inability to cross the bridge between New Jersey and Pennsylvania as she drove to her friend's house in the Poconos. This was looked at in a more symbolic way but, nevertheless, as a transition from one place to another. Many people have difficulty traversing "troubled waters," and a bridge is often considered a symbol in terms of a change from one state of being to another, which can exacerbate our fear of the unknown. We know what we know and are comfortable with routine. We are often not comfortable with what we don't know.

After some time in therapy, Rosemary began to see that her greatest fear was of the fear itself. With the help of mindfulness treatment, Rosemary began to take life one day at a time, sometimes one hour at a time. Her attention to the present took her mind off her catastrophic thinking, which then allowed her to manage short blocks of time instead of projecting way into the future. She began to minimize the what-ifs and was more practical about the here and now. And she also realized she actually did possess the skills she needed to live her life in a more comfortable way. Now, Rosemary is driving wherever she wants to, has less fear of dying, and reports that the quality of her life is greatly improved. Although Rosemary could have benefitted from coming into therapy sooner, she was strong and determined enough to forge ahead to conquer her debilitating anxiety.

In all the cases discussed above, each individual entered therapy in search of solutions to their problems. But did they enter therapy at the right time? I have noticed that some tend to avoid therapy when in a crisis. I have heard, "I'm too stressed out to come to therapy" and "My life is so crazy now I can't come in" and "I'm feeling depressed; when I feel better, I'll call you." If you ask me, it would be exactly the right time to call a therapist when you're feeling stressed, when life is driving you crazy, or when you are depressed. Yes, people who feel good can also benefit from therapy, but the right time to seek help is when you are not feeling well. I cannot make this point strongly enough. I am hoping the people who read this book will consider coming into therapy sooner rather than later. You will be happier and healthier for it.

# Chapter 5

# Depression

## Not What Everyone Thinks It Is

Depression is probably the most known of mental-health issues, but it is arguably the most misunderstood. Depression is classified as a mood disorder. When we are not in a good mood, we proclaim we are sad, unhappy, "blue," or "under the weather." We can feel sad, unhappy, or glum and not necessarily be depressed; however, depression usually encompasses these same words. How can this be? And what exactly is depression?

Depression is considered a biologically based disorder, which means the root cause of depression is based on biological factors, such as a depletion of the neurotransmitter serotonin (the "happy" chemical) between the nerve cells, or neurons, in the brain. Without getting too technical, our brain cells "talk" to each other with chemicals that travel from one cell to another since our brain cells or neurons do not actually touch one another. The gap between cells is called a synapse, and this is where certain chemicals travel to before being absorbed back into their original cell. This secretion and reuptake goes back and forth as signals travel through our brain. Sometimes there are not enough chemicals, like serotonin or dopamine, in the synapses, or they are reabsorbed too quickly for the effect to be felt.

This is where antidepressant medicine helps slow down the reuptake of these "feel good" chemicals so they remain in the synapse longer, thus producing a brighter mood. There are many types of antidepressants that can affect different neurotransmitters in the brain. Because there is a wide range of biological factors, including metabolism, weight, and tolerance of or intolerance to certain medicines, people respond differently to the various antidepressants. A doctor may need to try several different kinds of antidepressants before a positive effect is seen. Most people will show an improvement in their mood after about two to four weeks on a medicine after a certain level of medicine is reached within the system.

However, a stigma still exists regarding the taking of medicine for depression, and many people will choose to not take psychotropic medication so as to not look "weak" (believing that they can will themselves out of depression) or be seen as "crazy." Ultimately, a person needs to make up his or her own mind about taking an antidepressant. It is important to note that this class of medicine has come a long way in increasing efficacy and reducing side effects. It can be quite miraculous to see a person go from being depressed and hopeless to opening up like a flower and finding a more peaceful sense of existence.

The criteria according to the *Diagnostic and Statistical Manual of Mental Disorders, Fifth Edition* for a major depressive episode are as follows:

1. Depressed mood for most of the day, nearly every day, as indicated by subjective reporting (e.g. feels sad or empty) or observations made by others (e.g. appears tearful). In children and adolescents can be an irritable mood.

2. Markedly diminished interest or pleasure in all, or almost all, activities most of the day, nearly every day (as indicated by subjective or observational reporting)

3. Significant weight loss when not dieting or weight gain or decrease in appetite nearly every day

4. Insomnia or hypersomnia nearly every day

5. Psychomotor agitation or retardation nearly every day (observational data)

6. Fatigue or loss of energy nearly every day

7. Feelings of worthlessness or excessive or inappropriate guilt nearly every day

8. Diminished ability to think or concentrate, or indecisiveness, nearly every day

9. Recurrent thoughts of death, recurrent suicidal ideation with or without a specific plan[2]

According to the DSM-V, if a person has five or more of the preceding symptoms during a two-week period, which is a variation from previous functioning, the person may be suffering from depression. As noted above, these symptoms can be reported either subjectively (by the person themselves) or observationally (from others) to meet the criteria. Exclusionary criteria may be a medical condition, substance abuse, or bereavement after the loss of a loved one. Some who are depressed try to "self-medicate" with alcohol or drugs as a way to feel better.

## Examples of DSM-V Criteria

Let's take a closer look at some examples from the DSM-V criteria that provide a greater understanding of what depression looks like. It is often difficult to say a person is depressed by looking at just one criterion. As noted above, it takes five or more criteria to diagnose someone with depression, and, unfortunately, it may take a combination of factors to determine that a person is truly depressed. However, as we try to determine when it's time to call a therapist for you or a loved one, getting into treatment *early* is always the right time to seek help.

1. Depressed mood most of the day, nearly every day, as indicated by either a subjective report or an observation made by others. Someone may report they are feeling sad or empty for no apparent reason. In other words, they may indicate that nothing bad has happened to change their mood. Also, someone may view the person as being upset and on the verge of tears, and when asked what's wrong, the person may report that they do not

know why they are so upset. Conversely, a person may report situational depression and be able to describe what is making them so sad. The death of a loved one, the loss of a job, and a divorce can all be the cause of a situational depressive episode.

2. Markedly diminished interest or pleasure in all, or almost all, activities most of the day, nearly every day. Examples may include not engaging in favorite activities (i.e., guitar playing), trouble reading, disinterest in a favorite TV show, or withdrawing from a sport they once enjoyed playing. Also, if someone seems to be isolating from people whose company they once enjoyed, this could be a sign they are depressed.

3. Significant weight loss when not dieting or weight gain, or decrease or increase in appetite nearly every day. When someone is depressed, they may not feel like eating or even have the strength to eat, which may manifest in weight loss. Conversely, if someone is in a depressive state, they may eat more than usual as a way to "soothe" their pain. Overeating highly caloric foods and snacks may be the only thing that brings the sufferer any pleasure, and they may engage in this unhealthy activity which, in all likelihood, will cause weight gain. This "coping strategy" may, in the end, only add to one's depression in that their unwanted weight gain ultimately makes the person feel worse about themselves.

4. Insomnia or hypersomnia nearly every day. One may know they are sleeping too much, but they do not have the energy to get out of bed. Someone observing this behavior may get angry at the sufferer and think they are willfully avoiding work and other responsibilities and just want to sleep the day away. This cannot be further from the truth. Staying in bed all day is not fun, and the person who cannot get up and function wishes they could shed their fatigue and do more with their day. Some folks may not be able to sleep at all or turn their thinking off when they go to bed and may also feel agitated at bedtime. These folks are

exhausted because of their lack of sleep and the discomfort of not being able to rest can be a painful experience.

5. Psychomotor agitation or retardation (the speeding up or slowing down of thoughts and physical movements) nearly every day (observable by others, not merely subjective feelings). This may manifest during the middle of the day or at bedtime. Someone who is restless may not know what to do with him/herself and may find they cannot sit still for any length of time. Others may find themselves listless during the day and lack the ability to even get up to get their mail, let alone open it.

6. Fatigue or loss of energy nearly every day. This may preclude one from getting involved in any task they once engaged in. The feeling of moving in slow motion in a world that seems like it's moving at one hundred miles per hour is not a good feeling, especially when one believes they cannot keep up in the world.

7. Feelings of worthlessness or excessive or inappropriate guilt nearly every day. These feelings can lead to a downward spiral that sucks any positive feelings someone may have about themselves right out of them. These negative thoughts are not only "heavy" to carry around but are dangerous, as a person may begin to feel they don't deserve to live. These "dark" thoughts may be compounded by other dark thoughts that can form the basis of how one feels about themselves and may preclude them from getting help if they do not feel worthy of getting into treatment. This can be one's subjective interpretation of themselves, or they may hear negative comments from others who do not understand how they really feel.

8. Diminished ability to think or concentrate, or indecisiveness, nearly every day. This can affect a person who may not have enough energy to focus or make simple decisions in their life. When someone is depressed, any effort, even thinking, can be difficult because the sufferer often lacks the energy to engage in these tasks. You may hear this person say, "I don't know" to even

the simplest of questions because coming up with an answer is difficult for them. Those not suffering from depression may think the depressed person is trying to avoid engaging them when, in actuality, they just don't have the energy to even put their thoughts together.

9. Recurrent thoughts of death (not just the fear of dying), recurrent suicidal ideation without a specific plan, or a suicidal attempt or a specific plan for committing suicide. Life may seem unbearable, and some people may feel unworthy of living and that they are a burden to others. They have no desire, energy, or reason to go on. Some will keep these thoughts to themselves; some will verbalize their pain. When someone who is depressed reaches this point, they may be thinking of what a relief it would be to not have to suffer anymore and may begin to plan to engage in suicide. The thought of making a plan to hurt themselves may actually give them a sense that there is a way out, and they may actually manifest some positive signs to friends or loved ones that may be misinterpreted to mean that they are getting better. However, these are false signs of improvement, and this is why the depressed individual should be in treatment with a psychiatrist and a therapist. In some cases, the depressed person may need to go to the hospital, where they can get around-the-clock observation and treatment. Hospitalization is not a sign of failure but of strength, where an individual chooses to get help rather than end their life.[3]

Please note: This book is not meant to assess, diagnose, or treat anyone with medical, emotional, or psychiatric problems. If you are experiencing any physical or mental-health issues, have thoughts of suicide, and believe you need help, either go to your nearest emergency room or call 911 immediately.

## More Than Just the Blues

Depression is more than just feeling unhappy or sad; it is a constant state of indescribable heaviness that is difficult to quantify. Dysthymia, or a "low-level" state of feeling blue, is different than a major depressive disorder. Those who are dysthymic may be sluggish and not appear very joyful, but they are able to interact with others, go to work, and are generally able to function and take care of their needs, albeit not at a high level. These folks can remain in this state for some time, and even though they believe they could be happier, many do not seek help and merely trudge through life one day at a time.

Depression is a much more serious illness. Someone who is depressed is in a constant state of anxiety and dread. They cannot feel joy and begin to withdraw from others who are happy because it hurts too much to be around them. Someone who is clinically depressed or having a major depressive episode feels like they are in a "bubble" and are "different" from everyone else. They believe they are insignificant, valueless, hopeless, and not worth the trouble to fix.

Those who are depressed may not get much sleep and wake up in the morning feeling exhausted. Others get too much sleep yet may still not feel refreshed. It is an ever-constant state of being fatigued from which there is no escape. Imagine having twenty-pound sand-bags attached to each leg and arm and trying to have a normal day. It feels like a nightmare to exist in a fatigued state and have the weight of the world on you as well.

Someone who is depressed not only feels different from everyone else but will act differently from others, too. Those who are not depressed exude an air of lightness and confidence, knowing that if they make a mistake it's not the end of the world. Depressed individuals have zero confidence and constantly worry about making mistakes, which puts their anxiety level into overdrive. They constantly worry about what they will do if something doesn't go exactly right. The combination of being exhausted and having to work so hard to get everything right is a recipe for serious trouble and, unfortunately, may lead to thoughts of suicide.

Being clinically depressed is like being in a state of paralysis. Not only is the body depleted of any energy, the mind is exhausted as well. Thinking hurts, and the prospect of ever feeling better seems a million miles away. Imagine having a toothache of the mind; the pain is constant, and tears are just a millimeter below the surface. It is a psychological, cognitive, physical, social, and spiritual illness that unless experienced is hard to imagine.

Too many depressed individuals do not seek help, believing that their depression cannot be treated. And many others do not want to see a psychiatrist for fear they will be labeled as crazy. Too often, those battling depression avoid medications that may be helpful. "I am not a pill person" they say. Others believe medication will change them in such a way that they may not know themselves anymore. Still others believe that if they have to take medicine it solidifies the fact that something must be wrong with them; therefore, if they don't take medication, it proves nothing is wrong with them.

There is so much erroneous information out there, including on the internet, that in order to help some people, trust and education are required that fact may be distinguished from fiction. Trust is a major factor when one goes to see a therapist or a psychiatrist. It's difficult to trust even a professional with many years of training and experience when someone has embedded beliefs against therapy and doctors (i.e., "My father didn't believe in going to doctors, so why should I?") Again, education is key for people who are resistant to treatment, with the hope that the depressed individual will begin to challenge their old belief systems and try something different in hopes of feeling better. Depression can alter positive thinking, which is why it is so difficult to help the depressed to help themselves.

## My Personal Experience with Depression

I became depressed at about the age of ten, as mentioned earlier, when I had to leave my friends and all that I knew after my parents decided to move out of the City to the suburbs. Although geographically the move was only five or six miles north, it seemed like a different world with a totally different mentality. Every aspect of life was different as I tried to assimilate from a kid with a city state of mind to the sub-urbs of middle- to upper middle-class neighbors and friends. I was angry, hurt, and lonely after the move, even though I made new friends pretty quickly. With a cascade of confusing and conflicting feelings and a change in culture, I felt I was on my own in navigating this new terrain without a guidebook or instructor.

From the beginning, I felt like an outsider, like someone who was different than everyone else. The sense of self I had in the old neigh-borhood was suddenly gone as I struggled to find where I fit in. I became apathetic and angry and acted in defiance toward my studies. I went from the top of my class in the city to near the bottom in my new environment. My mood became progressively more depressed as I finished my middle-school years. Teachers were even surreptitiously referring to me as the "melancholy" one, which brought a chuckle in the classroom from the kids who guessed it was me. I believed the school system was against me, and with some of the kids at school and even the teachers labeling me, my depressed state worsened.

High school wasn't much better. Although my friends from the neighborhood and from the previous school year were continuing on to the local high school with me, I had no goals, no ambition, and no desire to even be in school. And my grades reflected my apathy. I just went through the motions without feeling or caring about much at all. Where all the kids who were thinking about going on to college were doing well in their classes, learning new languages, playing after-school sports, and participating in clubs, I basically just came home after school, went to my room, and maybe talked to a few friends on the phone at night. Not having any goals for the future further deep-ened my depression. I relied on my friends for answers to questions I had about life after high school and life in general, as I viewed them as "parental" figures. Needless to say, I did not rely on my parents much outside of the basics required to live. I considered my friends my "real" family, and I felt safe and comfortable around them.

After high school, I saw some of my friends go off to college and get jobs. I remained anxious, depressed, and apathetic on a daily basis. I also had an underlying feeling of anger that at times was not easy to control. I was confused and, now, looking back, I believe my anger stemmed from the fact that I was not prepared for life as an adult. My parents encouraged me to get a good job with benefits, but nothing they suggested appealed to me. I knew I could do more with my life, but it took a while for me to muster the courage to sign up for a few college courses and to begin another chapter in my life. Yet, I still didn't feel better—until I entered therapy and later saw a doctor for medication. If I'd known how therapy would change my life in such a tremendous way, I would have started the process much, much sooner.

Having been a client in therapy many years ago and now, as a therapist, I have experienced both perspectives in relation to the therapy process. This is invaluable in my work as a therapist, and I encourage anyone considering getting into the area of mental health to be a client themselves, not only for the experience but to work through whatever they may be struggling with. I have had clients who avoided therapy (and medication) for quite some time before beginning the process. The cases outlined below illustrate how therapy can help, especially with those who suffer from depression.

## Deciding on Medication—Francis

Francis was a married woman in her mid-sixties with no children who worked for a successful company as a staff nurse within a health-care setting. According to Francis, she had been deliberating as to whether or not to enter therapy for issues surrounding her marriage, her elderly mother, her job, and a basic unhappiness with life for some time. Francis was not an easy client. She was angry, obstinate, and negative about her life and would often sprinkle our sessions with colorful words and phrases that actually fit well into our dialogue.

Regarding her marriage, Francis indicated that she and her husband were like many couples who had been married for forty years or more in that they seemed like ships that passed in the night, without saying much to one another anymore. The couple reportedly tolerated each other's quirks, but they also tuned each other out when they were together.

Francis's elderly mother lived alone in a house she once shared with her husband, but she was reaching the point where her independence was being questioned, as evidenced by the food rotting in the refrigerator, her unkempt house, and questionable hygiene issues that were obvious to everyone but her.

Francis described her job as boring, and she outwardly wondered why she had spent the last thirty-two years there. She felt neutral about her job and like she had just been going through the motions for many, many years. And she often wondered if her struggles were worth all the effort she put into her mundane, unhappy life.

We discussed her issues on a weekly basis. Each session, Francis would come into the office with a list of complaints, interspersed with a litany of expletives, about work, family, home life, and her mother. Francis was particularly upset about the fact that she was getting older and was questioning whether she could continue living her life this way.

Francis began to see suicide as a way out, and so her behaviors were constantly monitored, and we made an agreement that she would call me if her urges became too strong. I talked to Francis about medication and indicated that I worked with a couple of psychiatrists who could help her. Francis made it clear she was not interested in going on "nut pills" because she didn't consider herself crazy but just someone who needed to sort through a few issues in her life.

Francis believed she was making progress and reported that she looked forward to our sessions. However, as much progress Francis felt she was making, she was actually stuck and unable to move beyond the issues for which she originally came to therapy. Often, I would recommend that Francis make an appointment to see a psychiatrist, but she would always balk and change the topic.

About two years into our work together, something changed. Francis finally realized that although she had been feeling better since entering therapy, in order to get to the next level, she needed to try medication. The thinking at the time was if she didn't feel better or if she felt worse, she could simply stop taking the medication, no harm done. The rationale was that at least we could say she'd tried.

Francis made an appointment with a psychiatrist I recommended and was diagnosed as having depression and given a prescription for a common antidepressant. The doctor wanted her to start slowly, increasing to a therapeutic dose over time. Francis was compliant with treatment, and over the months, after each doctor's visit, she increased the dosage a small amount at a time. At about the second month, I began to see a change in Francis. Her mood was brighter, and she appeared calmer. She did not go off to the races with disparaging comments toward her mother, husband, or colleagues, and had a softer tone. She reported sleeping better and having an improved appetite. What I was witnessing was a "new" Francis who knew she was changing in a positive way. Her rough edges were becoming smoother and, most importantly, her talk of suicide had faded away.

Over time, Francis took on a more philosophical view of having an elderly mother, of getting older herself, and of her career in health care, which she agreed had actually been a good one. And Francis continued to grow. When a managerial position opened at work, Francis talked about applying for it. When I first met Francis, she was sick of her job, sick of her family, and sick of life. But after about three years in therapy and being medication compliant, she actually believed in herself enough to apply for the job. And she got it! Francis had always been a front-line health-care worker, and now she was part of the management team.

She was so happy with her progress that during one session she actually said, "How come you didn't get me to try medication sooner?" We both had a good laugh at her rhetorical question and ended the session with a better-late-than-never understanding. When was the right time for Francis to call a therapist? According to Francis, it should have been sooner, but oftentimes getting into therapy is a decision that takes a certain amount soul-searching before one reaches out for help.

*Bipolar Disorder—Beth*

Beth, married and with children, came to me after she had been written up for the third time in twelve months for both performance and behavioral issues at her job as a licensed practical nurse. Beth reported that she had gone to her workplace employee assistance program for short-term treatment after her second write-up, where she was mandated to do so by her boss for essentially the same issues. Now seeing the writing on the wall, Beth decided to commit to therapy to try to understand her issues and save her job.

Beth had already been seeing a psychiatrist for bipolar disorder and was reportedly medication compliant with her mood stabilizers and antidepressants. Although she took her medication every day, she experienced bouts of hypomania (a state of increased energy) and depression and would have her medication adjusted for whatever episode she was currently experiencing.

When Beth was hypomanic, she would become more provocative in her behaviors, especially sexually, and when she was depressed, she had thoughts of leaving her job, divorcing her husband, or even of suicide as a means to end her emotional pain. Beth's mood swings had been noticed by others, particularly at work, where she was labeled "moody" by coworkers who did not know she was bipolar. Beth would start to badmouth her colleagues and criticize them for their poor performance, which paradoxically negatively affected her own performance. And Beth would make promises to her boss and colleagues on work projects she could not fulfill.

Beth's relationships were often fraught with poor judgment to the point where the other staff members had to eventually block her phone number so that she would not harass them. At times, Beth would indicate her desire to sleep with a particular colleague she erroneously thought felt the same way about her. And at home, Beth accused her husband of spending money they did not have only to later realize that she was the one who'd actually spent the money.

The worst part about Beth's depression was when she would talk about how hard her day-to-day life could be and that she was not sure she wanted to live like that anymore. Beth was aware that when she was depressed, she would begin to have thoughts of wanting to hurt herself. I encouraged her to be honest in our sessions when thoughts like this occurred and told her she could call me in between sessions if she was feeling particularly vulnerable. This agreement seemed to be the safety-net Beth needed as it reassured her that help was just a phone call away.

Our work together was not easy. Although I found Beth charming and bright, I also saw through the illness as she tried to make logical sense of things when she was grandiose or in a depressive state. And she was good at trying to convince me. However, when Beth was hypomanic, I would point out her over-the-top thinking and how that thinking and the associated behavior could land her in trouble in and out of the work environment. We discussed how, when Beth was depressed, her most dreaded fears were more than likely overblown (it was my suspicion that Beth also suffered from borderline personality disorder) and that with skill building, she could manage those dark times.

We talked about her mood shifts in relation to her work-life balance, and we worked on building skills she could use if she began to feel "too good" or, conversely, "too bad." We also talked about the importance of seeing a psychiatrist on a regular basis, being medication compliant, and coming to therapy once a week if life became too stressful. Beth agreed to these terms. However, we acknowledged that it was not always easy to discern when she was hypomanic or depressed, because sometimes the shift was almost imperceptible. And we discussed how she could rely on my observations when she came to session as a guide to where her stability was on the continuum between being hypomanic and depressed. Beth found this strategy very helpful.

Another aspect of our therapy was that Beth had been a recovering alcoholic for ten years at the time we were working together. As she knew that her ongoing sobriety was something she needed to maintain, she was active in Alcoholics Anonymous, would go to meetings on a regular basis, and had a sponsor with whom she seemed to get along. However, poor judgment, relationship problems, and episodes of hypomania put her continued recovery at risk. At one point, Beth reported that she was not seeing eye to eye with her sponsor and that she'd abruptly "fired" her because she believed she was being too controlling. Another time, Beth indicated in session that she had struck up a "friendship" with a man who also attended the AA meetings. She later verbalized that she was beginning to have feelings for this person and that she was having a hard time not accepting his requests for her to sleep with him. Even though we discussed this issue in the sessions, she reported one day that she had indeed slept with this person only to feel guilty afterward.

Beth and I talked at length regarding her risky behavior and the negative consequences if she did not get her life back on track. And as she had in the past, Beth agreed that she had a lot to lose if she did not start to exercise better judgment. She subsequently found another sponsor she liked, and she decided not to go any further down the road of infidelity and consequently severed ties with her lover. I encouraged Beth to let her psychiatrist know about what had happened, which she agreed to do.

Though Beth's challenges with bipolar disorder had affected her since her early twenties, it wasn't until she was older that her manic and depressive episodes impacted her life in far more consequential ways. Although Beth reportedly had not been in therapy when she was younger, getting into therapy when she did not only seemed prudent but necessary in helping her manage her mental health. Did Beth get into therapy at the right time? It would probably have been more beneficial had she done so at a much earlier age to save herself from her risky behavior and some of the difficult memories she carries inside her.

*Stuck in Neutral—John*

John came to me after his psychiatrist thought it would be good for him to reconnect with a therapist to talk about his issues and hopefully get some traction with his life. John was in his fifties, had never married, and had been unhappy for some time. He had essentially been stuck for the better part of ten years, more than likely longer, when the company he had been working at for twenty plus years closed. As a "temporary" job, John went to work for a hospital as a valet, parking cars during the second shift. John reported that he never had any intentions to remain with the hospital in that capacity but claimed he had never gotten a break and had been discriminated against by potential employers because of his age. John was living in the basement of his childhood home, which he'd inherited with his brother.

John's story is not one of any great successes but rather maintaining, so that he would not regress and require hospitalization. Although by all accounts John was a functioning adult, he could not quite seem to attain the next level that would boost his confidence and bring more happiness to his life. John basically led a solitary life. He had no friends, did not see his relatives often, and was not close to anyone at work. He said he knew he should be doing more with his life but felt discouraged, which left him with very low self-esteem. John did very little to help his situation and cast blame on everyone else for the hole he was in, taking little responsibility for making his life better. It was difficult at times to see him struggle and to hear his repetitive mantra that no one would give him a chance. We came up with an action plan for him to fill out several job applications, but he returned to the next session and admitted he had not applied to any of the positions. His only comment was, "I guess I should have." Part of me wanted to be firm and hold John to the plan we had agreed upon; however, he was so sensitive and fragile I feared he may have left therapy and not come back.

John had a habit of shying away from people, especially in the work environment. After seeing John for some time, I became convinced that he suffered from not only depression but a personality disorder.

Personality disorders in the DSM-V are broken down into three distinct "clusters" that comprise close but different types of characterological disorders. I believed John fit into the cluster-A grouping and that he suffered from schizoid personality disorder. For example, cluster A encompasses odd and eccentric behaviors and, along with two other personality types, schizoid personality disorder's common features are social awkwardness and withdrawal. This disorder, along with the other cluster-A types, is also dominated by distorted thinking. People who fall into this category work jobs where they have the least contact with people (i.e., a night watchman or a bus driver on the graveyard shift). Even though John's work as a valet had him in contact with other people, the second shift gave him far less contact than if he worked during the day. And while parking cars, John spent little to no time with coworkers.

John's day look something like this: He would work the 3:00 p.m. to 11:30 p.m. shift at the hospital and then return home, where he would watch TV and have a couple beers before he went to bed. He would get up around 10:00 a.m., make some breakfast, run some errands, and do some work around the house or just watch TV. John would have a little lunch at around 2:00 p.m. before getting ready to start his workday over again. His work schedule and life actually ran counter to most people's nine-to-five schedules. John was just getting up when most people's workday was in full swing. When it approached quitting time for the daytime folks, John was barely into his shift. And as most were retiring for the evening, John was still at work for several more hours. John would work every other weekend as well, almost effectively precluding him from having any social time with the Monday-to-Friday nine-to-five-ers.

My work with John consisted of validating his progress no matter how little was achieved. We would brainstorm why something did not go as planned, and I would coach him to get more résumés out and point out when his thinking became distorted. I also tried to help him with his negative thinking. For example, when John would say no one wanted to hire him because of his age, I would try to help him see that age brought experience, which was something people just entering the workforce did not have. I even encouraged him to try a dating site with the hope that his ego would get a boost if he had a few interactions with women. Later John would report that no one had contacted him, but he also admitted he had not contacted any one either, thus seriously lowering his odds of meeting someone. John was afraid of reaching out and making the first move in his work life and personal life and expected that others would come to him with job offers or dates. This is what distorted thinking is all about.

John had been in and out of therapy for years and appeared to be medication compliant with his antidepressants and other meds. I believe John's depression was compounded by his personality disorder, which was introjected somewhere in his developmental years. His fear of others, low self-esteem, lack of confidence, and reported victimization translated into John blaming others instead of taking responsibility for his life. There reportedly was no history of abuse, but one has to wonder where and how all this came to be. When should John have called a therapist? He probably should have been in therapy from an early age, but, reportedly, his parents did not believe in talking to "strangers" about life's difficulties. I believe John thought he was trying his best but did not have the capacity to understand that he had it within him to be a more productive individual and to have his needs met without relying on external factors. He was the one who'd set his limitations and built a wall around himself as a self-protection mechanism that would not allow anyone in nor put him out there in what he perceived was a dangerous world.

John's condition would become alarming when he would periodically verbalize that he was tired of failure and did not see the point of going on anymore. In session, we would talk about his negative thoughts and how being more proactive could help him develop more confidence and self-esteem. John would seem to take the advice, but when asked in the next session if he had proactively done anything to help his situation, he would say, "Not really" with no valid reason why. John eventually dropped out of therapy, and even repeated calls could not bring him back. Perhaps if John had been able to set aside his fears, false beliefs, and his "poor me" attitude, he would have climbed another rung on the ladder and proven that hard work pays off. The hope is that John will once again enter therapy and be able to meet some of his unrealized goals.

## Suicide

The information presented here is not intended to assess, diagnose, or treat anyone with suicidal ideation. It is meant to be used for informative and educational purposes. If you have thoughts about wanting to hurt yourself in any way, call 911 or go to your nearest emergency room. Once stable, calling a therapist for ongoing psychotherapy would be a prudent decision.

I cannot talk about depression without also talking about how negative thinking, hopelessness, helplessness, feeling like there are no other options, and feeling alone, trapped, and anxious can be the start of the downward spiral toward taking one's own life. Chronic depression and suicide are insidious, as these types of negative feelings can overtake a person without warning. Although suicide is often associated with someone who has lost everything in life and is at the end of their rope, may individuals who commit suicide seem to have it all together. People from all walks of life, even the wealthy and famous, have died at their own hands, their loved ones and fans left to wonder why.

Suicide is something not often talked about. When someone commits suicide, people find themselves in shock and trying to find explanations about what caused the event. People understand that if someone has cancer, treated or not, there is a chance they may not recover. But depression is still not often viewed the same way. If suicide can be looked at as a symptom of an illness of the brain, it makes sense that if someone does not get the appropriate treatment, they can become sick and die. Still, it is much easier to understand the course of an illness caused by cancer, and people will talk openly about it, while depression is not very well understood and, in many cases, is only discussed in whispered tones or behind closed doors.

Even though our society has come a long way in eliminating the stigma around mental illness, it is still not a topic people can easily talk about outside the medical community. Part of the problem is that if someone has a terminal disease, it often manifests outwardly in the form of changes in weight, hair loss, and a deterioration of the body that cannot be ignored. With depression, the "deterioration" happens on the inside and is not so obvious to the average person. A sad example is that of comedian Robin Williams, whom many thought was a happy and content individual. Certainly the public saw him as the quintessential comedian who had fame and wealth and everything for which to live. Many have come forward to report that Robin Williams had been depressed for years, but others believe that his worsening Parkinson's and that the disease dementia with Lewy bodies (DLB) led to his suicide. Others have speculated that his worsening medical condition made him depressed, which in turn led him to take his own life. Whatever the exact sequences of events, the fact remains that depression played a significant role in his death.

According to the American Foundation for Suicide Prevention, suicide is the tenth leading cause of death in the United States. Forty-four thousand people die each year by suicide (121 per day), and for every successful suicide, twenty-five are attempted. The rate of suicide is the highest in middle-age (45–64 years of age) and by white men in particular. Men kill themselves 3.5 times more often than women, but women have more attempted suicides. And firearms account for about 50 percent of all deaths. There are estimates that upward of one million people engage in intentionally inflicted self-harm every year. Veterans have the highest suicide rate, at approximately 20 a day, with vets having a 21-percent higher rate than adult civilians. Contributing to this high number of suicides is a condition called post-traumatic stress disorder, which is not only associated to war but any traumatizing event one experiences in their life.

## Post-Traumatic Stress Disorder (PTSD)

Post-traumatic stress disorder (PTSD), classified as an anxiety disorder, is the development of disabling psychological symptoms following a traumatic event. This disorder was first identified during World War I, when soldiers who returned home from the war experienced chronic anxiety, flashbacks, and nightmares for weeks, months, and even years following their tour of duty. At the time, it was known as "shell shock." Post-traumatic stress disorder can occur in anyone who has experienced severe trauma outside the normal range of human experience. Trauma such as a plane crash, being in war, having survived an earthquake or other natural disaster, rape, assault, and other violent crimes can produce intense fear, terror, and a sense of not being in control of one's life. Common symptoms after the trauma may include:

- ◉ nightmares about the event
- ◉ feelings of detachment from others
- ◉ loss of interest in activities that once brought pleasure
- ◉ intense anxiety
- ◉ difficulty sleeping
- ◉ poor concentration
- ◉ outbursts of anger
- ◉ emotional numbness
- ◉ the avoidance of activities associated with the trauma
- ◉ impulsivity

- ◉ intense flashbacks of the trauma
- ◉ repetitive and distressing thoughts about the event

Post-traumatic stress disorder can affect people of any age who suffer from fear, loss, and perhaps guilt surrounding the original trauma. Although PTSD is listed under anxiety disorders, many people with this condition self-medicate with alcohol and drugs as a way to cope; however, this negative coping strategy can lead to depression, which may increase the risk of suicide.

---

When should someone suffering from PTSD call a therapist? For veterans, keeping a close connection with the Veterans Administration (VA) seems evident; however, the fact that 70 percent of the vets who commit suicide were not regular users of the VA's services is disconcerting. For civilians of any age, when any trauma occurs that alters one's psychological growth and well-being, leaving them feeling sad, despondent, and hopeless, or when others begin to notice a negative change in mood and a reduction in socialization, or when thoughts that life is too difficult to go on and a suicidal plan is being formed—if any of these events, criteria, thoughts or behaviors occur, these people should call 911 or go to their nearest emergency room immediately. There is help close by.

# Chapter 6

---

# Anger Management

*Controlling a Difficult Emotion*

W e all get angry. Like frustration, disappointment, sadness, and fear, anger is a common emotion. It is not a "bad" emotion; we can actually learn a lot about our environment and ourselves when we feel angry. However, some inappropriately express their anger by acting out with rage and violence, and that's when it becomes problematic. Often, we verbally communicate our anger to let someone know they've done something to upset us. For example, just before going on vacation, a woman asked her husband if he would do the laundry, which he agreed to do. When the wife arrived home and saw that the laundry was not done, she became angry. They could have discussed this, and the husband could have explained why he hadn't done the laundry, but the wife flew into a rage, accusing the husband of being lazy, which set off a chain-reaction of arguing, eventually leading to threats of canceling the vacation. Obviously, talking about why the laundry was not done would have been better than threatening to cancel an expensive vacation.

The American Psychological Association offers two definitions of anger that I believe best describe this often-misunderstood emotion:

1. "Anger is an emotional state that varies in intensity from mild irritation to intense fury and rage" according to Charles Spielberger, PhD., a psychologist who specializes in the study of

anger. Like other emotions, it is accompanied by physiological and biological changes; when you get angry your heart rate and blood pressure go up as does the level of energy hormones adrenalin and noradrenaline. "Anger can be caused by both external and internal events. You could be angry at a specific person (such as a coworker or supervisor), or event (a traffic jam, a cancelled flight, etc.), or your anger can be caused by worrying or brooding about your past or current personal problems. Memories of traumatic or enraging events can also trigger angry feelings."[4]

2. "Anger is the emotional drive to defeat anyone or anything that we perceive as a threat" according to Israel Kalman, MS, a nationally renowned speaker on how we deal with anger. In "nature," anger is what we feel toward an enemy and is a way of helping us defeat our enemies. In nature, getting angry is the first step toward "winning" and often "surviving." In "civilization," getting angry becomes the first step in "losing" and may bring along a host of civil, legal, financial, and other serious problems. We will take a closer look at the problems anger can cause us later in the chapter.[5]

In the first definition, we find that anger can vary from "mild irritation to intense fury and rage." Anger can be triggered by external or internal events and traumatic memories. As we can see, anger is a systemic emotion that encompasses many different processes in our bodies. It can be manifested physiologically, biologically, psychologically, and behaviorally.

The second definition looks at anger in a more sociological way. It speaks of anger as being more of a survival mechanism in a modern "jungle," where we feel like we need to defend ourselves against a perceived threat. In "nature," anger can help us protect ourselves from a "saber-toothed tiger," but in "civilization" our anger, if expressed in an out-of-control manner, can get us into a lot of trouble.

## Different Styles of Anger

There are different anger "styles" people demonstrate. Poor communication habits can trigger anger, and certain behaviors in others can "push our buttons." However, there are skills that can be utilized before, during, and after an angry episode that can help keep emotions from escalating. For this next part, I would like to borrow material from the workbook *Stop the Anger Now*[6] by Ron Potter-Efron, MSW, PhD, an excellent resource for anyone looking to understand their anger in a more comprehensive way.

### *Suppression of Anger*

Like most emotions, anger can be demonstrated in a number of different styles. Those who deny their emotions suppress their anger because they are not comfortable with conflict. They believe that if they let their anger out, there will be a secondary issue—pushback from the receiver of the anger. Also, some people who stuff their anger are afraid of it, as well as themselves, and worry if the "genie is released from the bottle," they may express their anger excessively and not be able to control it. Suppression of any emotion can lead to many ailments, as emotions don't just go away. They tend to linger and, as mentioned, may manifest in physical, psychological, and behavioral ways. Like other emotions, anger can be expressed through thoughtful communication and does not have to reach a level of no return. When communicating with another person, "I" statements can be helpful; for example, "I feel angry when you say you are going to do something and you don't do it." By beginning the sentence with "I" instead of the accusatory "you," we take the blame off the other person, and a softer dialogue can unfold. When people blame others for their anger, they may say something like, "You always make me angry when you do/don't do that." That's what's called the "blame game," where the angry person puts their anger on the other person. Using "I" statements disarmingly explains the emotions a person may be experiencing. When we blame someone for our feelings, we are actually saying, "I have no control over my feelings and take no responsibility for them because you caused this." Blaming others for our feelings is not only inappropriate, it can often turn a benign conversation into a battle.

## Fear of Confrontation

Another style of anger is when a person "checks out" of the interaction. Those who withdraw are typically people who also do not like conflict, but unlike people who suppress their emotions, they tend to be passive-aggressive about expressing their anger. Someone who is passive-aggressive cannot express their anger directly to the source but will do it in a round-about way. For example, an employee may be angry at his boss but afraid to discuss the situation face-to-face. Since the employee won't say anything directly to his boss, he may surreptitiously key the boss's car in the parking lot to release his anger. Or a woman who is angry at a friend for not inviting her to a party may "accidently" be late to a movie she ostensibly wanted to see. In both examples, the angry person "withdraws" from expressing their anger directly, expressing it in a behind-the-back manner instead.

## Anger Addiction

The next anger style is identified as anger "addiction." This type of anger produces a "high" when a person is full of rage. For those who are chronically angry, this "rush" of adrenaline is like taking a drug. Adrenaline can give the body energy and a feeling of invincibility and power that's pleasurable for some. Those who are chronically angry crave these feelings and can get "hooked" on them. Who doesn't want to feel powerful, confident, and in control of their life? In reality, however, a person who is addicted to anger is actually out-of-control, has little self-confidence, and certainly no respect for others as they act out their aggression. These folks need to stop hiding behind their intimidation tactics and come to terms with their behavior.

*Manipulators*

People who manipulate others are a breed all to themselves. Not only will they fuel the fire with someone, they will actually bring a third person into the argument to help support their position. For example, a wife may be angry at her husband, then recruit their son so that mother and son team up against father. The problem with this is that the son hears only one side of the argument, his mother's. And she, acting as the gatekeeper of information, has the power to morph the details to win over the son to her side. This tactic can be detrimental, splitting the family and causing severe turmoil as family members form unhealthy alliances.

*Exploders*

Sometimes people who are insecure and want to be intimidating use the tactic of exploding to express anger. Arguments that escalate to this point can turn into physical altercations where people get hurt or worse. Those who are so angry they explode may punch, hit, slap, kick, push, choke, use a weapon, and sometimes kill their targets. Oftentimes a child may come to the rescue of a parent who is being abused and get hurt too. Seeing this kind of violence in the home may instill in children that there is a normalcy to this behavior, and they may carry it into future relationships. Girls in these types of families may have difficulty setting limits with a boyfriend because of the lack of boundaries they witness in the home. Family members feel they have to walk on eggshells so as to not trigger a violent outburst from an explosive parent or caregiver. This can lead to stress and anxiety as the family members never know when and what will set someone off. Children may also feel ashamed of their families and will not bring friends to the house for fear they and their friends will be subjected to a parent's wrath. Chronic, out-of-control anger can destroy families, break apart relationships, put jobs in jeopardy, and invite legal problems if not addressed in therapy.

## Communication Habits That Can Fuel Anger

We learn at an early age how to communicate with other people. Someone transmits a message to us (whether in the form of a question or statement), and we respond. As we get older, we understand that there are certain nuances to communication that form a more complex dialogue between two people. Words can be used to bring forth ideas, thoughts, and feelings to help two (or more) people understand each other. The content of what is being communicated may differ depending on the context in which it is delivered. For example, in a work-training session, the communicator is usually the group facilitator and the one who does most of the talking, aside from any questions a group member may have. In a meeting with the CEO of the company, there is usually a message to be delivered to everyone in attendance, and the CEO may be the only one talking. In a brainstorming group, everyone in attendance may deliver their thoughts at any time as free-floating, spontaneous ideas. In a religious observance, the minister or preacher is usually the one who delivers a message to the congregation without any dialogue occurring. We can see by these examples that active communication comes in different forms in different settings.

However, most communication occurs between two people or in small groups of people (i.e., a family, staff members, etc.). It is in these types of interactions that we learn how to speak, what to say, and when to say things to form back-and-forth communication. But sometimes free-flowing communication becomes problematic. For example, sometimes people talk in a stream-of-consciousness manner, without any punctuation, thus disallowing the other person a chance to speak. This not-giving-the-other-person-a-chance-to-talk style can create a form of apathy in the receiver, who may feel the person transmitting the communication doesn't care if the receiver has a chance to respond.

Constantly interrupting someone when they are trying to put their thoughts or ideas forward may be interpreted as disrespectful to the person talking and may generate anger in them. It is a social skill to know when to interject a thought after another person has finished talking. Someone who constantly interrupts others may either be minimally rude or so self-centered they're not aware they are even doing it.

If the transmitter of a message finds the receiver looking everywhere other than at the speaker, they may perceive disinterest on the part of the receiver. By not focusing on what a speaker is saying, a receiver can convey that the conversation is boring or a waste of their time. Showing impatience while someone is talking can also foster anger in the speaker.

Finishing the other person's story, explanation, or interpretation of information as a way to speed up the conversation is not only rude, but the person doing so can be erroneous in their assumptions as to where the story is going. The person giving the information should be given the courtesy of finishing before another person adds their thoughts to the dialogue.

Rephrasing someone's thoughts in a negative way or responding with sarcasm can also cause a speaker to get upset because it discounts the message given. Although ultimately we are in control of our own feelings, feeling disrespected in our interactions with others can trigger feelings of mild irritation to straight-out anger or rage toward the receiver.

## Behaviors That Can Push Buttons

There are many types of behavior that can fan a spark of irritation into a fire of anger. In this section we will look at behaviors that push others' "buttons," as well as the behavior aimed at us to push our "buttons." I like to think of a button as something we wear—like a doorbell that can be pushed—that sends an "electric current" down to a past, unresolved emotional trauma or the sensitive "scar tissue" of a partially healed psychic wound. So when we get angry, it's actually our own issues being triggered and not necessarily what the speaker actually means to convey. Someone can make a comment to one person and have no effect on that person whatsoever, while that same verbiage can send someone else into a fit of anger. That's why everyone has different sensitivities from the past and not every comment or statement will produce the same reaction in everyone. These behaviors can create feelings across the anger continuum, from mild irritation to explosive rage. Anger can also be a cover-up emotion that can hide hurt, shame, guilt, sadness, fear, and other feelings. Let's look at some of the behaviors that push our buttons or the buttons of others.

1. *Interrogation.* Have you ever experienced that rapid-fire questioning aimed to get at the "truth" behind your behavior? This includes questions such as "Where were you? Who were you with? What time did you get home? Why didn't you call?" and so on, with the hope of getting additional, previously withheld information from another person. When we interrogate others or are interrogated, a feeling of mistrust is engendered. The central message here is "I don't believe you, and I don't trust you," which can cause us to feel angry or hurt.

2. *Blame.* It's never fun to be the target of someone's suspicion when it's unmerited. It's unfair to ascribe ownership of a negative outcome to a suspected individual when we don't have all the facts. When we blame others, we disallow the likelihood that anything or anyone else could have caused something to go wrong or a problem to have developed. Blaming someone for a negative situation can be problematic, especially if all the facts have not been assessed. It is understandable for someone to become angry having been blamed for something, especially if they did not do it or have unknowingly taken part in an adverse outcome.

3. *The need to be right.* This becomes an issue when a person's ego is so big they cannot tolerate anyone else's perspective as being valid and they try to push their personal beliefs onto others, persisting to the point where others become angry. Everyone has their own opinions and beliefs about the workings of the world, but when someone tries to force their opinions upon us, it can engender disrespect and lead to heated arguing.

4. *Labeling.* It can be highly disparaging when someone openly believes something about us that is not true or only partially true: "Joe is the black sheep of the family," "Michael is a trouble-maker," "Sarah is a nut job." Derogatory labels can evoke anger in us, especially when the labeler tries to justify their belief; for example, someone calls a person a "wimp" for refusing to escalate a conflict. This labeling can anger the labeled person because it challenges their decision not to continue the disagreement. The labeler may feel that the label is justified, but, of course, just because someone chooses not to escalate a situation, it doesn't make them a weak person.

5. *Disrespect.* Have you ever run into someone who has no regard for anyone else's beliefs, values, principals, integrity, or work ethic? Many interpersonal conflicts escalate when someone feels they are being disrespected. Disrespect comes in many forms, though it may look different between cultures, ethnicities, races, sexual identities, and religious beliefs. When we feel disrespected, we may interpret the other person's words to mean "I don't care if I hurt you, disparage your name, or slander you," which is something most of us instinctively push back against. A person who feels disrespected may try to defend their "honor" in ways that may be problematic. We all want to be respected for who we are, and when another person tries to "muddy" our name, it's easy to feel angered.

6. *Threats.* A threat is commonly worded as an if-then statement and can be insulting and intimidating: "If you do such and such, I will . . ." or "If you don't do such and such, I will . . ." It's like giv-ing an order with negative consequences attached. A few exam-ples: "If you don't clean your room, I'm taking your cell phone away." "If you continue to come in late, you will get terminated," and "If you don't quit smoking, I'm leaving." The threat may or may not be carried out, but it's an ultimatum no one likes to hear and can lead to anger.

7. *Complaining.* It can be maddening when someone repeatedly verbalizes what's wrong in their life, yet they don't try to do anything about it. We have all heard people complain, and we have all complained about one thing or another, but it becomes a source of frustration when a complainer refuses to fix things. "My house is always a mess, and I can't find anything." Solution? Clean and declutter. Some folks will do their best to remedy a situation, but many others won't. They feel it's easier to keep complaining. "I hate my job. I dread going to work every day." Solution? Start looking for a new job. "My husband and I just don't talk to each other or have anything in common anymore." This is a tough one because the solution is not easily remedied. Divorce is an option, but the better route would be to get into therapy to see where the marriage started breaking down and work toward resolving the issues.

8. *Apathy.* It can trigger anger when we feel that another person just doesn't care about us or a problem we are experiencing. We all appreciate it when someone listens to us and acknowledges our troubles. But hurt feelings, often masked by anger, can arise when we feel like someone just doesn't care about us and cannot appreciate what we are going through. And it causes that much more pain when we expect a friend, family member, or loved one to show concern and they don't. When we believe that others just don't care about us, we may not be there for them when they need support, thus perpetuating a cycle of hurt and resentment.

9. *Mind reading.* It's frustrating when someone assumes they know what we are thinking or planning to do when in fact they are way off the mark. Assumptions are tricky because they are built on bits of fact we may have about someone's intentions, but we can never fully know what a person is thinking or planning to do without actually asking them. The person who is trying to mind read or assume what another person is going to do is, in effect, only

guessing about the person's future behavior. To have someone try to guess what we are going to do and then share that assumption with others is inaccurate at best and could be dangerous at worst. Mind reading is closely related to believing a rumor; in both cases, a complete story can be formed on very little information, and often the story is riddled with inaccuracies. Mind reading, assumptions, and rumors can have major implications in the workplace: "I heard John found another company and is planning to leave the firm"; with one's marriage, "Someone told me Jane is having an affair with her boss"; and upon one's reputation: "I heard Harold was able to buy that big house through questionable business dealings." Mind-reading assumptions can cause confusion, pain, embarrassment, and anger. The simple solution is to ask questions in order to ascertain the truth rather than just guessing at what might be going on. However, it would be wise to avoid personal or sensitive subjects that could produce an angry response.

10. *Emotional punishment.* This button-pusher comes in several different forms. Someone may tell us how we should feel in a particular situation; for example: "You shouldn't feel that way; it was just a joke." Another form of emotional punishment is when someone cannot discuss a situation calmly and yells at their target. This may be a way to intimidate and blame them and not give them a chance to say anything, as shown in this example: "Every time you do that, you drive me crazy!" How can you respond to that? A third way to punish someone emotionally is to give them the silent treatment and chose not to talk about a problem, leaving the other person in the dark about how the silent one is really feeling. These three forms of emotional punishment can push our buttons and perhaps trigger emotions based on a past trauma initiated by a parent or caregiver during childhood. Feelings of anger, hurt, disappointment, guilt, and shame can come boiling up when similar behavior is being acted out in the here and now.

These are just a few of the behaviors that can push our buttons or the buttons of others. Everyone has sensitive areas or wounds that can instantly spark an emotional reaction. This can be surprising to the person experiencing the feeling; they may be unaware of the depth of their wound as well as to the person who knowingly or unknowingly triggered that response.

---

When is it time to call a therapist? When past trauma is causing current problems in relationships, the work setting, at home, or in social settings. If not treated, these "wounds" will persist and can perpetuate one's hurt and fear. Self-awareness and delicate work with a caring therapist can help give one insight into their anger problems. The sooner help is sought, the earlier the healing can begin.

---

### Anger Management:
### How to Avoid, Manage, and Move Beyond Chronic Anger

This next discussion centers on the three phases of anger originated by Ron Potter-Efron. I borrow from his workbook, *Stop the Anger Now*,[7] samples of material on the importance of what I will refer to as the beginning, middle, and end phases of anger.

We all have buttons, or triggers, that can initiate an angry outburst or rageful behavior. If we are lucky enough to know what sets us off, we can use prevention skills to lower the chances that we will react to something or someone in an angry way. Controlling our anger is not always easy, though, because our responses are often based on a multitude of factors, such as our upbringing, our thoughts, and our feelings (from the past or present), our actions and behaviors, and on situations that touch on our principals, values, and spiritual beliefs. Anger, like many of our other emotions, is very complex.

When we consider ways to prevent anger, we must first and foremost be self-aware and come to understand how the potential for anger may occur. Where we go, who we encounter, the state of our body and mind, and what skills we can draw from to mitigate anger are important in countering anger before it escalates. And to that point, do we always have to choose anger when we become upset, or can we decide not to get angry? I have found it can be a choice. For example, while driving home from work one day in bumper-to-bumper traffic, I looked around at other drivers to see how they were handling the situation. Some were talking on the phone, some appeared to be listening to the radio, and others were just calmly waiting for the traffic to start moving again. However, I also noticed drivers who appeared quite upset. Some were leaning on their horns, hoping that their frustration and noise would force the traffic to move. Someone else was trying to edge their way around the other cars to get a car length or two farther ahead, which would, ostensibly, bring them to their destination sooner. And someone else was yelling out their window at a driver who was not going to let him enter the lane. Interestingly, it was the same place, time, and situation for everyone, but the reactions were different for many of the drivers. Did some choose to not get angry, and did others choose to let their anger be known? It seems like if we couldn't control our emotions, everyone would be angry. And for those who believe getting angry is not in their control, are they not being responsible for their own internal turmoil? This is just one of the possibilities to consider when we notice our anger starting to manifest.

*Self-Awareness*

One factor to consider is this—we know what others do to us to get us angry, but do we ever consider what we do to others to get them angry? I believe everyone can justify why they get angry. It may be that some people think, "He did this, and she didn't do that, and it wasn't supposed to turn out this way, and I deserved that more than he did." When we feel wronged, we get angry. But what might *we* do that may irk someone or prod them into getting upset with us? Do we justify that we are right all the time and others have no business getting angry, or do we have the ability to see that our words and behaviors can also offend and upset others? It's not easy to admit that we are wrong and that we may have unknowingly (and sometimes knowingly) pushed someone's button. Thinking about how others see us and how our words and behaviors may affect them is one way of managing our anger.

## Trigger Thoughts

Another area of self-awareness is learning to recognize our "trigger thoughts," or thoughts we preload in our minds when going into an interaction with another person. For example, if you have a negative thought just before going into a meeting with the boss, who wants to discuss an error in a project, that thought may quickly escalate into a negative outward reaction. Thoughts such as "You are always criticizing my work, and I don't like it" or "I'm getting tired of being pulled into your office every time a problem arises" can prime us for an angry outburst. It would be better to go into the meeting with a clear and present mindset that minimizes the possibility of sparking an angry encounter and prevents an already sensitive issue from becoming something much bigger.

## Having a Clear Head

Making a personal decision to not talk to anyone about an important topic when you're tired, not feeling well, or impaired by alcohol or drugs (including some prescription medications) is certainly a wise decision and can minimize the potential of angry interactions. When we are not thinking clearly, our words may not come out the way we intend, or we may make the mistake of telling others "how we really feel," which often can lead to devastating consequences. Some people use alcohol or drugs to give themselves a false sense of courage when engaging with others. This approach leaves the person impaired as it can lower inhibitions and disengage "filters" and promote misunderstanding or lead to anger or aggression. It's can be hard enough to think clearly when we are rested, feeling well, and sober. Having some or all of these negative factors in place and trying to think straight can be all but impossible.

## Developing Insight

Developing insight regarding our thoughts and behaviors in how they relate to the emotion of anger is an essential part of self-mastery. Are we aware of our physical responses as anger is developing? Everyone has a uniquely individual response to anger. Learning to identify the first inklings of physical uneasiness can give us a clue that we are moving toward anger. Some people notice that their heart begins to race as their anger increases. Others notice a clenching of the teeth or a tightening of the muscles just before their anger starts to rise. Some begin feel warm, or "hot under the collar." Being in tune with how our bodies react when we start to feel agitated can help us avoid potential problems.

## Reality

We like to believe that we have a lot of control in our lives when, in fact, we probably have less than we think. There are many factors that are out of our control—other people, the time, the weather, the future, and many other situations large and small. This is called reality. For some, the inability to control their world fosters perpetual underlying feelings of anger. Knowing that not everything in life is in our control is a good place to start to embrace reality. If we can work toward accepting this concept, perhaps we can live a more peaceful existence and not feel so uptight and angry every time something doesn't go our way.

## When Anger Is Unavoidable

There are times we cannot prevent anger but may need to manage it. The good news is that we can learn to manage it. If we can be aware that we are beginning to get angry, argumentative, or enraged, there may still be time to control it. One tried-and-true skill to deescalate anger is to simply walk away from a situation. Sometimes we know that if we continue to butt heads with a spouse, a child, a boss, or anyone else, it will escalate into something out of control. If we can be alert to what is transpiring in the present moment, if no other skill is employed or working, we can simply walk away and come back to the issue another time. It may seem like a cop-out to leave an argument, but if there is no progress being made or if the situation is escalating, leaving is the better choice. It can be our undoing if we stick around and try to "win" when in actuality we can lose in a big way.

## Don't Make It Worse

Another aspect of preventing or suppressing anger is simple to understand when cool heads prevail but difficult to do when in the heat of an argument. Sometimes we may be so sure we are right about a given situation that we dismiss any possibility that we could be wrong. As bad as a situation may be, the one thing we don't want to do is make it worse by jumping to conclusions. A simple argument can turn into a name-calling event with hurtful consequences that last for weeks, if not longer. Without good judgment and giving others the benefit of the doubt, a dispute with a neighbor can turn a friend into an enemy, and disagreements at work can lead to termination. Anger, if not managed, can have dire consequences in our lives.

## Healing from Anger

We live in an imperfect world, and sometimes, in spite of our best efforts, anger gets the better of us, leaving wounded hearts and spirits in its wake. When that happens, it's comforting to know that things can be made right again. When those involved in an angry entanglement have had a chance to cool down and the thinking is clearer, we can begin to reverse our sense that the other person is the "enemy" and find more peaceful ways to move forward. Here are some possible action steps to start the healing process:

◎ We can apologize and take responsibility for our part, even if the other person is not ready to concede their part in the disagreement.

◎ We can acknowledge that the other person actually possesses good qualities that were eclipsed by the argument.

◎ We can communicate with the other person in "I" statements, which allows us to take ownership of how we feel without blaming others. For example, we can say, "I feel angry when you don't listen to me" as opposed to "You make me angry when you don't listen to me." The difference here is communicating our own feelings and not blaming someone else for causing our anger. Communication can be the key in resolving conflict in any area of our lives and may actually produce a stronger bond with the honesty conveyed.

However, in some cases, anger can be vocalized so strongly and hurtfully that recovery may take time, if it occurs at all. In the work environment, an intense exchange with one's boss may cost a person their job, especially if it was a repeated offense. A line crossed between friends and family may be so severe that those relationships are never the same. And in the healing between loved ones, couples, and spouses, it may take some time for trust to be restored. It may be easy for someone to walk away from a relationship that was once built on love if they were badly hurt, and some should. But if there is a sense that mutual respect can be replenished through necessary work in a therapeutic environment, that would be the first step in the healing process. Understanding how to manage anger and gaining insight into the etiology of anger can bring about growth, maturity, and responsibility for those with anger issues.

*Compromise*

I was once working with a couple when the subject of compromising came up. The wife was agreeable to compromising on their key issues, but the husband was not. He was so sure he was right in their arguments, he actually said, "I consider a compromise 'losing,' and I will not compromise." This was the first time I heard a spouse communicate this in a session. The wife verbalized the unfairness in her husband's statement and looked to me for guidance. I asked the husband if he was willing to give a little to quell their constant arguing, and he said he wasn't. The wife pointed out that his controlling nature was exactly what was wrong with their marriage. Other couples I have worked with both agreed that compromise was a worthwhile avenue to explore in helping their relationship. In this particular case, the husband was unwilling to budge an inch, and it was no surprise that the wife soon filed divorce papers.

## Forgiveness: A Panacea for Anger

Finally, there is a method of healing many discount but which may be one of the most powerful tools in overcoming the negative effects of anger. Learning to forgive can often resolve problematic, episodic anger. More importantly, it can play a significant role in easing the pain that often accompanies anger-based interactions. At face value, forgiveness may seem a logical and simplistic approach; however, for many, it is almost an impossibility. To forgive someone after an egregious act has occurred takes strength, fortitude, and courage. Why should someone forgive another person who has hurt them immensely? Shouldn't they seek revenge and vengeance? Many people feel that way. However, others find closure and peace in forgiving, which allows them to be able to move forward. Those who forgive don't condone the behavior that occurred. They have a strong sense that everyone is inherently good but that certain circumstances have led someone down the wrong path. Whether to forgive or not forgive is certainly a personal decision, but people who forgive report a sense of closure in their nightmarish situations.

Overall, anger is a complex emotion that can help us identify certain "dangers" in our environment. It can also help us pinpoint childhood "wounds" that may still be raw and need healing years later. But anger can also become an out-of-control emotion if we do not understand the triggers that can escalate a confrontation. Anger-management therapy can be of benefit to anyone who wants to understand the genesis of this strong emotion.

When is it right to call a therapist? It's when anger begins to draw the attention of our coworkers, teachers, spouses, friends, family, and sometimes law enforcement. It is always beneficial to begin therapy as early as possible, but if you've waited, beginning therapy when you become aware that the problem needs to be addressed is prudent. Everyone gets angry, but anger does not have to become unmanageable when it comes to those we work with, those we love, and even strangers.

Chapter 7

# Substance Abuse

## *Destructive on Every Level*

So far we've talked how important it is to call a therapist early on regarding anxiety, depression, anger management, and for other issues. It's just as important to seek help as soon as possible when it comes to substance abuse to prevent the downward spiral it so often causes. Although we never want to see someone we love get involved in drug use, addiction is insidious and most often occurs swiftly and stealthily. Those who abuse drugs usually get to the point where they become too far into their addiction to stop on their own and require intensive treatment. Opioids, legal or otherwise; cocaine, crack, molly, and other designer drugs; methamphetamine; and other mind-altering substances can be highly addictive and deadly. No one in their right mind wants to be chained to a drug or overdose or die, but as the reader will learn, tens of thousands lose their lives to drug abuse each year. Alcohol is also an addictive substance and taken to excess can also cause death.

This chapter is not meant to diagnose or treat substance abuse. This information is presented in the hope that it will bring awareness regarding the dangers of using drugs and alcohol. This chapter looks into the many treatment options available to help the user turn their life around at any point in their disease. Also, it's often the case that a substance-use disorder may have an underlying mental illness where the user is attempting to self-medicate. No matter the underlying cause, the combination of drug use and mental-health issues is a prevalent problem today. If you are aware that you are trying to drink or drug your pain away, seek help immediately!

## Opioids / Pain Medication

Currently, substance abuse, especially that of opioids, is ravaging the country as never before. People of all ages, genders, races, religions, sexual orientation, and socioeconomic status are susceptible to the dangers of both legal medications that are abused and illegal street drugs. Some of the legal opioid medications that are abused are oxycodone, Oxycontin, Percocet, Vicodin, fentanyl, Dilaudid, codeine, and Demerol. These drugs, when used as prescribed, can alleviate the pain caused by cancer, surgery, and chronic ailments. Leftover medications like these can be found in medicine cabinets and stolen without the person for whom the prescription was written even being aware that they are missing.

Once these prescription medications run out, users will seek them out on the street, which is expensive, or go directly to cheap heroin. There are many street names for heroin, but some of the more common are dope, smack, H, horse, and black tar. Often, packets of heroin are stamped with a name or picture to help the user identify where to buy it again. Many have described the opioid or heroin high as "a warm feeling that envelopes the body like a comforting blanket" followed by what is described as similar to the "afterglow" of a sexual experience; however, the extreme first-time experience can never be replicated, and heroin users who attempt to capture that same experience find it falls short each time. Users quickly develop a tolerance for the drug, which causes them to require more and more heroin to get high. Some users can work their way up to thirty, forty, and even fifty bags of heroin a day. They become hooked and need the heroin to alleviate the withdrawal symptoms that occur if more of the drug is not taken. Many compare the feeling of withdrawal to the worst flu they have ever had. Others describe feeling like their bones are being broken, terrible cramping and severe diarrhea, vomiting, and anxiety and restlessness leading to a complete lack of functioning. The addict continues to use to ward off these terrible physical and psychological states, but in the process they are only building a higher and higher tolerance for the drug.

*Fentanyl*

People are overdosing and dying at an alarming rate due to the use of synthetic fentanyl and other drugs mixed with heroin. It's estimated that sixty thousand to seventy thousand die every year from opioid overdose, eclipsing deaths from firearms and car accidents combined. Knowingly or unknowingly, substance abusers are buying what they believe is heroin, but later, often when it is too late, they realize that the drug was spiked with fentanyl. Many of these addicts, even after overdosing, will go back to the same dealer because they believe that "good" product will give them the best high. However, that product may end up killing them.

Since the advent of the reversal medication Narcan (Naloxone, patented by Sankyo in 1961), some of these overdose victims are able to "reverse" and are revived. Naloxone works by "scrubbing" the opioid receptor sites clean of any opioids. A person can be saved if the EMTs or police get to them in time and if they are able to incrementally administer doses that provide a safe and successful reversal. Immediate withdrawal symptoms may occur, including sweating, shaking, nausea, vomiting, trembling, flushing, and headaches. Sadly, a reversed individual will sometimes become combative and not realize how close they were from exiting this world and will demand they be discharged from the hospital only to go out and use again.

## Benzodiazepines/Depressants

Benzodiazepines, also known as benzos, downers, or tranks, on the street are another class of prescription medication often abused. Benzodiazepines, including Xanax, Klonopin, Atavin, and Librium, fall under the category of depressants and are primarily used to treat anxiety, help manage anxiety attacks, and can help a person coming off alcohol to mitigate withdrawal symptoms and seizures. However, when abused and doses are taken that would not normally be prescribed, the user can experience respiration depression, dizziness, reduced concentration, anxiety, and cravings for more of the drug. Benzodiazepines that are short acting and enter and leave the body quickly are the most addictive. Once this occurs over and over, the body begins to build a tolerance and more of the drug is needed to produce the same effect.

## Barbiturates

Barbiturates, including Amytal, Nembutal, phenobarbital, and others (also known as barbs, bennies, and yellow jackets on the street) are another class of depressants used in sleep medications, to treat anxiety, seizures in epilepsy, and as an adjunct to anesthesia. Because the dosing between a safe administration and a lethal one is so close, barbiturates have mostly been replaced with other, safer medications. As with benzodiazepines, barbiturates are highly addictive, and the abuser can quickly develop a tolerance for the drugs. Because barbiturates depress respiration, a person can die once their respiration is severely arrested. Users are not doctors and are often unaware of the danger they put themselves in when they abuse these medications. Taking these drugs in combination with other drugs and/or alcohol increases the likelihood of the user becoming unconscious or dying. Due to the current flooding of cheap and powerful opioids such as heroin, many deaths from benzodiazepines and barbiturates are probably underreported. Nevertheless, when these and other drugs are abused, the risk of self-injury and death increases many times over.

*Stimulants/Amphetamines*

Another class of prescription medications is stimulants, such as amphetamines and methylphenidate. Common brand names are Adderall, Concerta, Vyvance, and Ritalin. Illegal names are uppers, speed, and black beauties. In medicine, these are used to treat children, adolescents, and adults for attention deficit/hyperactivity disorder (ADHD) and have been prescribed to college students to help them be more attentive in their studies. Paradoxically, this class of stimulants has an effect of helping individuals become more "focused" in their tasks while also producing a calming effect on their behavior. Other uses for stimulants are obesity, impulse control, asthma, and nasal congestion. However, when Adderall is taken in doses above what was prescribed, users can experience symptoms such as headaches, nausea, restlessness, and a pounding heart. Abuse of Adderall can produce increased tolerance, dependency, and addiction. In higher doses, symptoms such as paranoia, mania, seizures, and slurred speech can occur. Even higher doses can cause cardiovascular issues, hypertension, hallucinations, unconsciousness, and coma. Mixing these with alcohol can mask the effects of the alcohol, thus making alcohol poisoning likely. Sudden death has been reported when misusing and overdosing on these stimulants.

### Illegal Stimulants

Illegal stimulants include cocaine, methamphetamine, and crystal meth. Cocaine is produced using coca leaves and processed in remote jungle labs primarily in Bolivia, Peru, and Columbia. Street names include coke, snow, blow, and nose candy. Cocaine is an intense, euphoria-producing stimulant drug with strong addictive potential. It can be snorted, smoked (crack), and injected, and mixed with heroin, the combination called a speedball. The effect of cocaine has been described as a rush of exhilaration and euphoria that can be experienced over and over in rapid cycles until one's supply runs out. Feelings of depression follow and prompt the user to use again. Other nonpleasurable side effects include restlessness, anxiety, and irritability. "Crack" is cocaine processed to form "rocks." It has been said that the difference between cocaine and crack is socioeconomic in nature. Cocaine is seen as a "rich kids" drug, while crack is viewed as an inner-city drug based on its lower price. In whatever form cocaine is used, its potential for addiction is high, and the damage to the body and mind, along with social and family problems, increases with continued use.

## Methamphetamine

Methamphetamine and crystal meth are basically the same drug, only methamphetamine is manufactured in a pill or powder form and crystal meth in slightly blue-white glass-like crystals. Both drugs can be manufactured illegally, but methamphetamine can be used legally in the form of Adderall, Ritalin, and Desoxyn—medications for patients with ADD and ADHD. It has also been used in weight-loss products. On the street, these drugs are called crank, ice, crystal, and poor-man's cocaine. Small meth labs are set up across the country in homes, apartments, and in various hidden spaces. Most meth or crystal meth is made in large quantities by Mexican drug cartels. The drug can be swallowed, snorted, smoked, and injected. Those who smoke or inject it report a brief, intense sensation, or rush. Oral ingestion produces a long-lasting high instead of a rush, which reportedly can last half a day. Both the rush and the high are believed to result from the release of very high levels of the neurotransmitter dopamine into the areas of the brain that regulate feelings of pleasure. Long-term meth use results in many damaging effects, including addiction. Chronic meth users exhibit violent behavior, anxiety, confusion, insomnia, and psychotic episodes that include paranoia, aggression, visual and auditory hallucinations, mood disturbances, and delusions, such as the sensation of insects crawling on or under the skin. Suicidal or homicidal thoughts are common, as well as sudden death, stroke, and organ problems. Since this drug is made with battery acid as one of the ingredients, chronic use can cause blisters on the lips and face, open wounds on the body, and "gummy bear" teeth, which can all render an individual unrecognizable. All drugs can be dangerous, but the total destructive power of meth and crystal meth is second to none.

## Marijuana

There probably hasn't been as much controversy over a drug as there has been about marijuana. As of this writing (2018), there are thirty-one states where medical marijuana, such as Marinol, can be used legally and twenty-two where marijuana has either been decriminalized or is legal for recreational use. Marijuana comes from the *cannabis sativa* plant, with THC (delta-9-tetrahydrocannabinol), which produces the psychoactive, or "high" effect. Marijuana is a dry, shredded, green-brown mix of flowers, stems, seeds, and leaves and can resemble tobacco in appearance. Common slang terms include grass, weed, ganja, pot, Mary Jane, and 420. Marijuana became popularized in the 1960s and was an integral part of the youth culture of the time, of the Vietnam War, and of the social changes across the nation. Marijuana has been "demonized" since the 1930s, with films such a *Reefer Madness* depicting people going "crazy" after smoking. Marijuana was embraced by the younger generation as their drug of choice versus their parents' "old fogey" cocktails, such as highballs, martinis, and whisky sours.

To get the active ingredient THC into the body, it is typically smoked in joints (marijuana cigarettes), blunts (a cigar devoid of its tobacco and refilled with the drug), pipes, bongs, and water pipes, but it can also be eaten in food or made into a tea. Marijuana extracts have been made using chemical solvents that draw out the psychoactive compound THC. Hash oil, honey oil, wax, and shatter are some of the names this form of the drug is known by.

When a person smokes marijuana, THC quickly passes from the lungs, to the bloodstream, and then to the brain, where the drug attaches to receptors that produce the high. Other effects include altered senses, difficulty thinking or problem-solving, and impaired memory. High doses can produce hallucinations, delusions, and psychosis, or serious mental illness. Long-term effects may produce thinking, memory, and learning deficits, and studies have shown that continuous use from adolescence to adulthood produces a loss in IQ that may not return with cessation. Other health issues related to marijuana smoking include breathing problems due to irritated lungs, as well as lung infections, increased heartrate, and problems with child development during and after pregnancy, as it has been found in mothers' breast milk. Long-term marijuana use can often exacerbate many forms of mental illness, such as depression, anxiety, and schizophrenia, but, ironically, those suffering from a mental illness may use marijuana to "self-medicate" the symptoms of their psychiatric issues.

There has been much debate as to whether marijuana is a "gateway" drug to other, more harmful drugs. Teens experimenting with marijuana may be more inclined to try other drugs to see what they can experience; however, the majority of people who use marijuana do not go on to use "harder" drugs. That being said, marijuana growers have been able to produce marijuana with high levels of THC. People accustomed to smoking relatively mild marijuana can become overwhelmed by the higher THC levels and experience high anxiety and severe confusion. Also, variant forms of marijuana dosed with unknown chemicals can lead the user to paranoia, psychosis, agitation, violence, and self-harm. Spice, K2, and devil's weed are just a few of the many names for marijuana laced with chemicals. Many individuals are hospitalized for injuries sustained by these drugs, including for severe medical and psychiatric problems. Other social, relational, occupational, and legal problems that last far longer than the high can come from the use of these and other drugs.

*Hallucinogens*

Hallucinogens are a diverse group of drugs that alter one's perceptions (awareness of surrounding objects and conditions), thoughts, and feelings. Hallucinogens can change sensory awareness in that the user may see, hear, smell, taste, and feel profound distortions in their environment (i.e., users have reported being able to hear color and see music). Archeologists have found evidence of hallucinogenic use dating back to 400 BC in the spiritual rituals of the ancient Aztecs, South American indigenous populations, and in the Hindu culture.

Some hallucinogens are plant-based, while others are made in laboratories. A few common plant-based hallucinogens include ayahuasca (found in the bark of a vine), mescaline (found in the peyote cactus), psilocybin (found in certain mushrooms) and salva divinorum. Hallucinogens that are made in laboratories include LSD (d-Lysergic Acid Diethylamide), DMT (dimethyltryptamine), DXM (dextromethorphan; a cough suppressant), Ketamine (animal anesthetic), PCP (phencyclidine, used in the 1950s as a surgical anesthetic), and MDMA (3, 4 methylenedioxy-methamphetamine, once considered for use in psychotherapy). Slang terms for plant-based hallucinogens are tea, mesc, buttons, cactus, and shrooms. Slang for laboratory-made hallucinogens include acid, Blotter, Window Pane, Special K, and Angel Dust. All drugs with potential for abuse alter one's consciousness and perception, but hallucinogens arguably change one's reality the most.

Although hallucinogens have been used for centuries, they came into their own in the 1960s with the youth of the so called "counterculture" who were influenced by leaders such as Harvard professor Timothy Leary, who preached to his followers to "tune in, turn on, and drop out."[8] He would encourage the youth of the day to go on "trips" to get a better understanding of themselves and the world in which they lived. Other "gurus" of the counterculture included scientists, psychiatrists, film producers, and actors. Much has been written about the "mind-expanding," insightful good trips many were experiencing, but there was also a flip side of "bad trips" that produced frightening episodes of terror. Users describe a "good" trip as a beautiful and colorful world filled with peace and love. Users on "bad" trips feel like they're being chased by the devil, see ugly facial distortions on themselves or others, and experience extreme paranoia from which they cannot escape. Short-term effects of hallucinogenic abuse may include a feeling of detachment from life, sleeping problems, loss of appetite, increased blood pressure, and psychotic experiences. Long-term effects of heavy hallucinogenic drug use are memory loss, anxiety, depression, and suicidal thinking. Experiences called "flashbacks," which are recurrences of a hallucinogenic trip even when no drugs are taken, can occur days, weeks, and months later, sometimes even longer. These out-of-the-blue episodes can be frightening, as the individual may not have any idea that a flashback has occurred and believe they are going crazy. Flashbacks can raise one's anxiety to where they can become hypervigilant to other flashbacks occurring. Physical problems can occur with hallucinogenic use, especially with the laboratory version of these drugs, including deleterious effects on one's internal organs, including the brain. Also, drugs such as PCP can cause seizures, coma, and death, and mushroom poisoning can occur if someone mistakenly consumes what is believed to be psilocybin, when in fact they are ingesting a poisonous mushroom.

Use of hallucinogens can be not only harmful to one physically but also psychologically. States of anxiety, depression, suicidal ideation, and psychosis can develop and persist.

## Alcohol

One of the most pervasive drugs around the world and in our culture is alcohol. Fermented grain, fruit juice, and honey have been used to make alcohol (ethyl alcohol or ethanol) for thousands of years. There is evidence of an early alcoholic drink in China around 7000 BC, and other fermented beverages existed in early Egyptian civilization for millennia. In India, an alcoholic beverage distilled from rice, called sura, was in use between 3000 and 2000 BC. Several Native American civilizations developed alcoholic beverages, the most notable from the Andes region of South America, which were made from corn, grapes, or apples and called chicha. In the sixteenth century, alcohol called spirits was used largely for medicinal purposes. Some thought that by drinking alcohol, "spirits" could enter the body to help "cure" the diseased. At the beginning of the eighteenth century, the British parliament passed a law encouraging the use of grain for distilling spirits for economic purposes. The nineteenth century brought a change in attitude, and the temperance movement in the United States began promoting the moderate use of alcohol, which ultimately became a push for total prohibition. In 1920, the United States passed a law prohibiting the manufacture, sale, and import and export of intoxicating liquors. During that time, the illegal alcohol trade was booming, and many consumed illegal alcohol in what were referred to as "speakeasies," or places where alcohol was illegally sold. By 1933, the prohibition of alcohol was nullified. Today, moderate use of alcohol is a part of our celebrations, social outings, and friendly gatherings. However, recent studies have shown that even modest amounts of alcohol produce deleterious health risks.[9] It would be prudent to keep any alcohol consumption to a minimum.

## Rock Bottom

Much has been written about the dangers of alcohol: the disease of addiction; physical, psychological, and spiritual decline; loss of relationships; loss of employment; and problems with the legal system. Numerous studies have been conducted on treatment outcomes, detoxification, rehabilitation, relapse prevention, and other preventative programs. Alcoholics Anonymous, Narcotics Anonymous, and Al-Anon (a program for families of alcoholics) meetings are found in almost every town across America. There is much help out there if the addicted person is ready for it. Yet even when one's life has been turned upside down by alcohol abuse, some are still not ready for help. This is probably the most difficult part of alcohol addiction for a loved one to witness—their son or daughter, mother or father, spouse or friend appears to be at "rock bottom" yet still may not be ready for treatment. Rock bottom is different for everyone; one person's lowest point may not be someone else's. Like all addictions, recovery lies in the readiness of the individual to step away from themselves to try to gain perspective on what the addiction is doing to their life. That many have been successful in extricating themselves from the hole of alcoholism breeds hope for others. Still, there are many who will languish for years or even decades before they are ready to seek help.

*Effects of Alcohol*

Physically, alcohol has the potential to damage the internal organs, such as the brain, heart, liver, pancreas, kidneys, and the immune system, which can ultimately disrupt bodily function. Many alcoholics are often malnourished due to poor diet or problems with their digestive tract. It has been shown that alcohol can cause esophageal cancer or cancer in other parts of the body. Psychologically, alcohol can lead to or stem from depression, anxiety, changes in mood or personality, psychosis, and suicidality. Since alcohol impairs one's ability to make sound decisions, many alcoholics who are depressed decide that suicide is the way out and act on their decision. Spiritually, those who are alcoholics (and other substance users) are said to have lost their way or have forgotten their purpose in life. They may feel there is something missing within them. They describe it as an empty hole. Instead of exploring to see what they are missing, substance abusers attempt to fill that hole or emptiness with drugs or alcohol. Temporarily, this may seem to work because the substances mask the pain, but when the drug wears off, the pain comes back and the pattern of use and misuse continues. Alcohol abuse can take a toll on a person on a number of different levels. Clearly, excessive and prolonged alcohol abuse can negatively affect one's entire life.

*Hard to Avoid*

Alcohol is so prolific in our society it is almost impossible to avoid. Advertisements in magazines, newspapers, and mailings, and on TV commercials, billboards, the radio, and the internet are prolific. As alcohol can be found in restaurants, sporting events, backyard barbeques, fund-raisers, wine clubs, work events, and even in Mommys' glasses at their kids' playdates, alcohol is ubiquitous. Liquor stores have "tastings" on Saturday afternoons so you can try before you buy, and they run classes on wine and single-malt whiskies and offer discounts if you buy in quantity. It's no wonder it's the number-one legal drug in America. If you drink enough in a bar, chances are the bartender will buy you a drink (probably to ensure a good tip) but may be unaware of your intoxication level when you leave to get into your car. From camping and fishing trips to ski lodges and white-water rafting to dining in restaurants around the world, alcohol is part of our lifestyle. How does one not drink? Drinking is a big part of business in that high-end dinners and expensive bottles of wine or liquor are given to clients to ensure future business and to communicate that their services are above their competition. Health-care professionals are wined and dined by pharmaceutical companies with the expectation that doctors will select their drugs over their competitors'. And when the average person buys a friend a drink across the bar, the gesture implies kinship. Alcohol can be used in many different forms, with different meanings attached it. But it can be insidious in that it can draw someone in without the person even knowing.

## Hidden in Plain Sight

There is a category of alcoholics referred to as "high-functioning." These individuals perform at a high level during the day but consume substantial amounts of alcohol outside work. These people may hide their alcoholism by producing quality work, thus masking the fact that they have an addiction. Many never suspect their boss or a high-ranking administrator has an alcohol problem, but others, such as the alcoholic's spouse or other family members, know. Children often witness and feel shame or embarrassment because of arguments between parents. Or one spouse may argue that the other never engages in activities or socializes like they used to because the alcoholic's real relationship is with the bottle. Couples often split up over this issue, but the alcoholic will continue their downward spiral, casting blame on the other so as to not take responsibility for their behavior. The children of alcoholics have been known to fall into a generational pattern of alcohol abuse, and the adult children of alcoholics have been known to experience a sense of loss due to the developmental "gaps" that occurred as their parent or parents were more invested in their drinking than nurturing their children through their formative years. Alcohol abuse can not only take a toll on one's current life but also on their children's future lives.

## Over the Counter (OTC) Substances

The list of drugs above is hardly exhaustive. There is also "huffing," which is the inhalation of chemical substances to get high. Products such as aerosol computer cleaners, gasoline, paint thinner, model-airplane glue, and various household products can be inhaled after being put into a paper or plastic bag or huffed directly from the container. This form of intoxication can make a person very sick and also lead to death.

Over-the-counter cold medicines are abused to produce an altered state of mind and hallucinogenic effects. Products such as Robitussin ("tussin") and Nyquil, when taken in large doses, can produce distortions in reality, a sense of euphoria, and dissociative effects (feeling disconnected with reality). When ingestion exceeds the recommended dosage, acute or chronic liver and kidney damage can occur and potentially lead to death. Psychosis, nightmares, anhedonia, panic attacks, tremors, hives, and a decreased respiratory rate are other symptoms of an overdose. Due to the high incidence abuse, pharmacies have had to sell this product from behind the counter to deter abusers from purchasing this medicine.

## Designer Drugs

Club drugs and designer drugs were brought into the party scene in the 1980s and 1990s at gatherings called "raves," in which these drugs were consumed so users could feel more into the lights and music and experience a connection with other party goers. These drugs include, but are not limited to, MDMA (3,4-methylenedioxymethamphetamine), also known as Ecstasy and Molly. Feelings of strong connection and "loving everyone" have been experienced at these "raves," which can last into the night. Users find themselves dancing for hours at a time, sweating profusely and becoming dehydrated. Since these drugs fall under the category of stimulants, a user's cardiovascular and respiratory systems can be adversely affected. Death can occur from any or all of these occurrences. Another drug that is not only dangerous but factors into criminal activity is Rohypnol, also known as roofies or the date-rape drug. This drug has been used to spike the drink of an unsuspecting individual, often a female, thus rendering her unconscious and allowing her "date" to take sexual advantage of her. When the woman awakens in the morning, she has no recollection of the rape occurring. Quaalude (ludes), Ketamine (Special K), and GHB (G) are the other drugs of abuse used at raves to induce a sense of belonging. These drugs can be dangerous in and of themselves but can be deadly when combined with alcohol or other drugs. A number of these drugs were once legal, and it has been up to law enforcement to catch up with the abuse. Crafty "chemists" who use their knowledge for the illegal manufacturing of drugs try to stay one step ahead of the law by making a slight change in molecular composition, thus changing its status from illegal to not illegal. Every time law enforcement catches on to the changes and adds the new drug to the illegal list, a new modification turns up. This cat-and-mouse game seems to be ongoing as illegal-drug manufacturers scramble to make a product that will retain their profits and keep them out of jail.

## Progressive Signs and Symptoms of Drug Abuse

Knowing and understanding the progressive signs and symptoms associated with drug and alcohol abuse can be useful in recognizing when someone needs help. Many of the signs listed below are interchangeable for drugs and alcohol (and to some extent other addictions), and the hope is that if someone begins to question their alcohol or sub-stance use, they will reach out to a therapist *before* severe problems occur in their lives.

1. *Cravings.* People experience intense urges for the drug as their addiction develops. Obsessing about the drug, purchasing the substance, and anticipating using are all part of cravings. Some have indicated that alcoholics have more of a "thinking" problem than a drinking problem because as physiological urges to drink develop, one's thinking about using prompts behaviors to drink. Cravings are a strong force, with many succumbing to their pull.

2. *Physical dependence.* A user's dependence on drugs or alcohol develops as they grow accustomed to the persistent presence and influence of the substance. Physiological and psychological disturbances occur when the drug is no longer in the system. An example of dependence would be taking a drug, such as a sleep aid, every night. The person may not be addicted to the medication, but they have grown accustomed to taking the drug to sleep, and without it, they may not be able to sleep. The body will know that the drug is not in one's system, and without that help to induce sleep, sleep will be intermittent at best. A slow tapering off the medication will allow the body to readjust to not having the medicine in the system.

3. *Tolerance.* Over time and with prolonged use, people build up a tolerance to alcohol or drugs, meaning they need more of the substance to achieve the same effect. As one drinks alcohol or uses drugs, the body adapts to the changes the substances pro-duce and actually expects the substances to be in the system. If a person continuously uses, the receptors in the brain sup-press the effects of the substances, thus requiring more of the drugs to produce the same effect. Also, with heavy and constant alcohol use, the liver produces more enzymes to break down the alcohol, disallowing much of it from getting into the blood-stream. A person will need more of the alcohol to get into the

system and actually "push through" the filtering process of the liver. It is not unheard of for someone's alcohol consumption to go from social drinking to addiction. The same holds true for drugs. Drug users have been known to go from using five bags of heroin to thirty bags and more a day. No one wants to be addicted to drugs or alcohol, but our biology and physiology wire us to require ever-increasing amounts of an addictive substance.

4. *Addiction.* Addiction occurs when the repeated use of drugs stimulates the brain's "reward circuit." When a drug is taken, dopamine is released, providing a pleasurable feeling, which in turn compels an individual to want to use again. As a person continues to use drugs, the brain adapts by reducing the ability of cells in the reward circuit to respond to it. This negates the high a person feels compared to when they first started using the drug. This is where tolerance develops and more and more of the drug is needed to try to get the same effect. Without constant and increasingly larger doses of the drug, withdrawal symptoms begin to develop, sometimes just a few hours after the last dose was taken.

5. *Withdrawal symptoms.* Some people experience withdrawal symptoms when they do not get their next "fix" or drink soon enough or when they attempt to stop using abruptly or wean themselves off the drugs over a period of time. It is the presence of a withdrawal syndrome that indicates physiological dependence is at play. In the acute stage of withdrawal, physical symptoms such as tremors, sweating, muscle aches, difficulty concentrating, nausea, vomiting, diarrhea, and cramping will occur. Withdrawing from alcohol and tranquilizers can produce the most dangerous withdrawal symptoms, including grand mal seizures, stroke, heart attack, hallucinations, and delirium tremens (a severe form of alcohol withdrawal that involves sudden and severe mental or nervous-system changes). In the

post-acute stage of withdrawal, emotional symptoms such as anxiety, restlessness, irritability, insomnia, depression, and social isolation are more common. It takes time for the brain to begin to normalize and heal, and for up to two years, the person in recovery may experience a roller coaster of emotions, sometimes on a day-to-day basis. It took time for the brain to get accustomed to drugs and alcohol being a "normal" presence in the system, and it takes time and perseverance for the brain to get back to a healthy state.

6. *Poor judgment.* When a person is addicted to drugs, he or she will often do anything to obtain more, including engaging in risky behaviors such as stealing, lying to friends and family, participating in unsafe sex, selling drugs, and engaging in various other kinds criminal activity. As the addiction grows, they get into financial trouble, neglect responsibilities, and become severely self-centered. During any period of the absence of drugs, when signs of withdrawal symptoms begin to set in, an addict will not think with reason but will focus only on how they can obtain more drugs to offset their impending sickness. Once this drug-seeking behavior takes hold, a person does not think about eating or sleeping and loses any sense of self-care; the only thought is on how to acquire more drugs. Being addicted to drugs can negatively affect every aspect of a user's life.

7. *Development of unhealthy relationships / isolation.* As a person begins to use more and more, their circle of friends changes. Healthy relationships fall to the wayside, and new "friends," more than likely users themselves, appear. These new friends share a commonality in their substance use that, in a sense, "normalizes" the user's behavior. Another aspect of drug use is social isolation, in which an addicted person my stop reaching out to family and friends. Instead, their drugs and alcohol become their "friends." They come to trust the addictive substance and feel they can rely on it to produce a consistent experience. This

convoluted thinking can drive an addicted person into further isolation.

## The Path to Recovery

Substance abuse and addiction are grim subjects, and when one is already ensnared, the situation can seem hopeless. However, while the best policy is to never start using or abusing any substance in the first place, with commitment and hard work, there are paths to healing. There are inpatient as well as outpatient treatment programs that can help an addicted person get clean and remain sober. Along with AA/NA meetings and regular sessions with a therapist, the chances for long-term recovery are good.

Often, an addict's behavior will spiral out of control to the point it necessitates a hospital admission. In the case of an overdose, police and EMTs try to revive the victim with Narcan (Naloxone), hoping to "reverse" the effects of the drugs. Sometimes the person who overdosed will be brought to an emergency room and given Narcan there. If (and *if* is the key word) an overdose victim is revived, a recovery specialist may come to talk to the person about long-term treatment. If the person won't agree to further treatment, they are free to leave the hospital once medically cleared. If the rescued person does opt for treatment, they will, in all likelihood, be sent to a detoxification program, followed by rehabilitation. Inpatient rehab is for those who have struggled with substance abuse for a long time or who may have overdosed a number of times and feel they are finally ready to leave drugs behind. It provides a safe environment with no distractions to treatment. Here they receive medical supervision around the clock and support from others also in recovery. Inpatient treatment may also provide group therapy, individual therapy, and in some facilities, exercise, yoga, and meditation classes. There is a higher likelihood of success if a person goes into residential treatment for twenty-one days or longer, depending on individual needs. Inpatient substance-abuse facilities are a powerful place for healing because of their team approach to treatment and because the patient is removed from the people, places, and things that caused them to start using in the first place.

Another way for a person to get substance treatment is a partial hospital treatment program, where the person comes to a facility during the day for group therapy, then goes home after the program. This type of treatment is for those who are less at risk for relapse than someone in a residential program. It allows them flexibility to manage their responsibilities at home or in the community. In this situation, although the drug of choice may be different, there is a commonality, with everyone seeking mutual support and discussing ways to avoid relapse.

There is a parable written by singer, songwriter, actress, and author Portia Nelson that speaks to the above scenario:

1. *I walk down the street and there is a deep hole. I fall in and I am lost and helpless. It isn't my fault and it takes forever for me to get out.*

2. *I walk down the street and there is a deep hole I pretend to not see. I fall in again and cannot believe that I am in the same place. But it's still not my fault and it still takes a long time to get out.*

3. *I walk down the street and I see that there is a big hole in the ground. I still fall in . . . it's a habit. My eyes are open and I know where I am. It's my fault and I get out of the hole immediately.*

4. *I walk down the street and see a big hole in the sidewalk. I walk around it.*

5. *I walk down another street.*[10]

This poem beautifully illustrates that we can go through life with our eyes closed and blame the world for our misfortunes, or we can take responsibility and make better decisions when we have insight and awareness. We can make the decision to not go down the path of using drugs and alcohol, but if we've already ventured in that direction, we can still seek help. What will the choice be?

Drugs are not only dangerous but can have a multitude of life-threatening consequences. Doing drugs can become one's education, job, career, and relationship, and other drug users can become ones "family." It is often difficult for the addicted person to see that they are falling into a chasm of hopelessness and despair. Family and friends may point out the seriousness of one's addiction, but often the substance abuser will ignore all the support and look at it as an intrusion in their life. People have been able to pull themselves away from their addiction through interventions, but the vast majority will continue on until they are ready to make a change, are forced to change due to legal problems, overdose, or die. On a more positive note, there are many dedicated and caring substance-abuse counselors who can help one try to move away from substance abuse and addiction. Detox, rehab, substance programs, AA/NA meetings, and other programs are out there to offer help, but your life will be on more solid ground if you make it a point to not bring drugs into your life at all. Once clean and sober, it would be wise to get into individual therapy to explore the underlying issues that may have precipitated the drug use.

Chapter 8

# Stress and Burnout

## Know Your Limits

*Generally, research . . . suggests that burnout, once it occurs, can lead to a host of medical issues . . . and errors in everyday life. It can be difficult to recover from. Thus it seems important to prevent burnout rather than wait for it to occur and then try to remediate it.*
*—Marsha Linehan, DBT Treatment of Borderline Personality Disorder[11]*

*Any idiot can face a crisis. . . . It's this day-to-day living that wears you out.*
*—Russian playwright Anton Chekov[12]*

The classic definition of stress is the response our bodies and minds have to the demands placed upon them and the *interpretations* we assign to those demands. Stress can actually force us to prioritize our tasks in a way that allows us to begin to tackle the most important work first, triggering adrenaline as a way to compensate for the perception that there's just too much on our plate and we do not have time to accomplish all our tasks. And when we begin to see the light at the end of the tunnel, we feel better when we know our situation was only temporary. Imagine planning a surprise birthday party for your spouse. You think about the phone calls you have to make, scheduling the event,

121

inviting the guests, buying and preparing the food or booking a reservation at a favorite restaurant, working hard to keep it a secret, and the countless other parts of planning a successful event. This can all produce stress. But once the party begins, you start to relax a little as you look around to see friends and family enjoying themselves. At the end of the party, you can finally sit down, put your feet up, and relish in the fun everyone had. Stress and anxiety built up to the time of the actual event, but in the end, everyone agreed that a great memory was made. Short-term pressure and mild anxiety, a task completed, and having a sense of satisfaction are the good parts of stress. But there is a not-so-good side that can cause great harm.

### Stress and Burnout

When we experience stress for an extended period of time without being able to alter, change, or ameliorate it, we can begin to feel empty, numb, devoid of motivation, hopeless, and beyond caring. Burnout is a state of emotional and physical exhaustion caused by excessive and prolonged stress.

The definition of burnout was first coined by psychologist Herbert Freudenberger in 1974, when he described it as "a depletion or exhaustion of a person's physical or mental resources attributed to his or her prolonged, yet unsuccessful striving toward unrealistic expectations, internally or externally derived."[13] Burnout is about not having enough energy, motivation, or passion. The thought is usually "I know it will never get better."

As you can see, there is a major distinction between stress and burnout—stress involves *too much* and burnout *not enough*. Everyone experiences stress in one form or another—in raising a child, in schoolwork, at our job, in having an ill family member, with financial pressures, in marital problems, with addiction, and with being homeless. Using the example of a homeless person, constant and prolonged stressors may include not having shelter in inclement weather, inadequate food, poor hygiene and medical problems, untreated mental illness, the risk of addiction, and encountering a bad element on the streets. In the face of the day-to-day, constant stressors of anxiety, depression, and in many cases post-traumatic stress disorder, with no end in sight, we can see how someone can turn from thinking that their situation is temporary and resolvable to the helpless and hopeless thoughts that being burned out can bring. Without some form of intervention, it's easy to see how someone can remain stuck, apathetic, and lack any physical or mental energy to change their situation.

However, not everyone's situation is as dire as someone who is homeless. Stress and burnout can also affect someone who is employed and appears, at least from the outside, to be doing well. Many jobs, including both blue- and white-collar jobs, come with a great deal of stress. Among other things, the stress can stem from the requirements of high-level performance, having to step up when a problem emerges, responsibility for staff productivity, and working in difficult environments, sometimes with difficult people. Those in the helping professions, especially doctors, social workers, nurses, and techs, are all prone to stress, burnout, and what is often called "caregiver fatigue." Those who work with complicated medical cases, with children and adolescents, with the elderly, with acute psychiatric patients, and with addicts, prisoners, and the abused and neglected are at high risk for burnout.

Who else is most vulnerable to burnout? Those who

- work exclusively with distressed persons
- are charged with the responsibility for too many individuals
- "personalize" their work
- have an inordinate need to save people
- are overly perfectionistic and idealistic
- feel guilty about their own needs
- work with others who are burned out
- experience a lack of appreciation by superiors, coworkers, and maybe even family
- have unrealistic goals that are daunting rather than motivating

- experience "vicarious" trauma (traumatized by another person's trauma)

No matter the situation, burnout can occur if you are lacking the awareness as to what all that stress is doing to you. Where most of these are familiar stressors, we don't often talk about the last—experiencing vicarious trauma. Let's take a look at that now.

### Absorbing Others' Trauma

Vicarious trauma (v T) is a condition particular to those who work in close contact with trauma survivors. In some cases, these people will empathically take on aspects of the trauma the survivor has experienced. This can result in symptoms similar to those of trauma survivors themselves. Making sure to prioritize self-care, maintenance of healthy boundaries with clients, and early detection of symptoms can all help to minimize or eliminate the onset of v T. Some questions to ask yourself when working with trauma survivors:

- Are you reexperiencing your own past traumatic events?
- Are you experiencing a blunting of affect, a numbing, a loss of feeling, or a tendency to avoid reminders of a past traumatic event?
- Do you have a heightened or exaggerated sense of being startled?
- Do you experience dramatic alterations in your outlook or worldview?
- Have you begun to demonstrate signs of antisocial behavior that were not present before working with your patient?
- Are your basic interpersonal relationships becoming dramatically affected?

One way to avoid vicarious trauma is to not personalize the work. It takes a lot of training and experience to work in a caregiving setting like a hospital or nursing home every day, but for some, being thrust into a new role they are not prepared for can lead to burnout. Many adults find themselves in the role of being caregivers to their parents. Some have the help of others or the resources to provide the necessary care, but others do not have that luxury and must do it alone. Too much stress without relief can lead to burnout, and if the caregiver becomes ill, who is going to take care of the two of them?

A person can get so burned out they become apathetic about everything, including self-care, which could lead to hospitalization. A person may get to the point where they not only become physically ill but emotionally ill as well. It is much easier to learn how to prioritize tasks, live one day at a time (sometimes one hour at a time), and discuss stress-reduction techniques than try to recover from burnout. If you find yourself headed for burnout from the constant barrage of stress, call a therapist now!

## Stress-Reducing Self-Care

When we talk about self-care, what thoughts come to mind? Eating right, getting enough sleep, and going to the gym? That's a great start, but it may not fix everything. Let's take a look at several areas of self-care that can help prevent burnout.

◉ How you are feeling, thinking, and behaving? Awareness of these things is key. Without introspection or insight, we can become robotic in our daily routine, just going through the motions regarding work, personal time, and our families. Even though it may be difficult to recover from burnout, it is not impossible, and an honest self-assessment will help you figure out how you became burned out in the first place. Without this knowledge, you risk repeating negative behaviors over and over again.

◉ How important is a comprehensive self-care plan to you? This is one of the first questions to ask yourself before getting started. Be honest with yourself and decide if now is the right time to start. Perhaps you are not ready yet. It may be better to know that you are not ready than to go into it half-heartedly and set yourself up for failure.

◉ How have past negative self-care experiences set habits in motion that may make present self-care challenging? If you have tried in the past to get on a path of self-care but did not succeed, what got in the way? A big part of self-care is being kind to yourself and not making your stress any worse than it already is.

◉ A healthy work-life balance is an important aspect of our overall health. What does your work-life balance look like? Our personal and work lives are both part our everyday lives. How do you know if you have a good balance? Do you spend too much time at the office in order to delay going home to an unhappy environment? Are you not motivated enough to live the kind of lifestyle you would like to live? Having a good work-life balance can enhance your life so you can be productive and have much-needed downtime as well.

◉ How do you process your "unfinished business" or baggage from the past so that you have energy for new challenges? Carrying the past around can drain you of the strength to embrace new experiences in the here and now. Get rid of the old to make room for the new. You will feel better for it.

◉ How and with whom do you spend your leisure time? Do you spend your leisure time doing what you really want to do and with whom you want to do it, or do you go with others' ideas of what you should be doing? It's better to be alone with your own company doing what you want than to be miserable doing things you really don't want to do with others. This distinction can be the difference between being happy or unhappy.

◎ How much quiet, or personal, time do you set aside for your-self each day? A lot of people feel that they cannot take some time for themselves and feel guilty just thinking about it. Every-one needs to "recharge their battery" and be alone with their thoughts, if only to stop, breathe, and feel the sunshine. That just may be enough to get you going again.

◎ Can you delegate some of your tasks? Do you have to do every-thing yourself, or can you ask for help? Some are afraid to ask for simple favors, but you'd be surprised how willing others are if you would only ask them for help. This action is the corner-stone of being assertive.

◎ Are you able to access resources that can help you manage your problems? No one can solve all their problems alone. If you find yourself in a situation and are not sure where to turn, can you find the resources to help guide you through the problem? Knowing where to look for help is just as important as knowing how to resolve issues yourself.

◎ A vacation away from home may be the start to finding peace within and to rest our tired body and mind. Not everyone can take a vacation, but vacations need not be expensive. The idea of going away, if only for a couple of nights, is to change the view from the same four walls you see day in and day out. A simple break can be enough to reassure yourself you are capable of relaxing and that in the future, you may be able to do more of it.

◎ Self-care is also about making decisions and you may need to make the biggest decision of all: to leave the job that is making you sick. Unfortunately, some people do not have the option to make a change like that, at least not immediately, but at least they should start a plan to leave. Just taking this proactive step can provide a sense of hope and empowerment. In some cases, people feel "stuck" in their jobs, which can add even more stress. If you find you dread going to work every day, whether it's because of a boss who is unfair, an overload of work, or employees who make the job environment a difficult place (or a combination of all three), it may be time (often it's past time), to begin looking for a position elsewhere. Your health depends on it.

The above list is certainly not exhaustive, but it will give you an idea of ways to cope with stress to avoid burnout. There are many areas of self-care where you can unwind and get the rest your body and mind needs to recharge. Burnout is a matter of recovery from a debilitating state of emptiness and exhaustion from which it takes time recover. A strategy I often recommend to my clients is to take life one day at a time or, even better, one hour at a time, breaking up the pressures we face into manageable chunks. It works for me! Give yourself the time you need to "detox" from the day-to-day "addiction" you experience every day. And remember to call a therapist as soon as you begin to feel overly stressed with everyday life.

# Chapter 9

# Problematic Interactions in the Workplace
## Where's the Teamwork?

The stress mentioned in the previous chapter was more self-inflicted in nature and pertained to how we view our workload and how we react to stress. This chapter takes a look at how the behavior of those who share work space can raise our stress levels and cause distractions, not to mention deleterious effects on our health and productivity.

In our work histories, we have all experienced bosses and coworkers who have made our jobs much more difficult than they need be. People bring to work their personal problems, anger, personality disorders, controlling behaviors, psychological problems, medical issues, addictions, family problems, and criminal and legal issues. These areas of dysfunction can manifest in the work place. If the list above seems worrisome, think about the fact that some people have co-occurring issues, meaning they have more than one problem with which they are trying to cope. Most people spend about one-third of their day at work, and those eight or so hours can either be productive and pleasant or unbearable. We will look at a number of difficult personalities, behaviors, and states of mind and then explore options on how you can deal with them in a productive manner, followed by how therapy can help you cope with difficult people in the workplace. I will borrow material from the book *Working with Difficult People* by Muriel Solomn,[14] as well as other business resources.

As always, it's better to seek counseling earlier than later, before an issue becomes much bigger. In a business environment, you can always start by contacting your company's employee assistance program (EAP) for free, confidential counseling services.

## Mean-Spirited People

Let's start with the tough guys—those mean-spirited folks who harass the people around them. They are threatening, hostile, and angry yet appear confident. They will try to control you through their words and actions. Mean-spirited people often recruit others to get support and to feel more powerful. I once heard of a group of employees in a particular hospital department who wore certain colors to show solidarity against other employees in the same department. This gang-like mentality existed until someone went to their supervisor. Human Resources got involved, but everyone wondered why it had reached a point where the intimidating behavior actually began to impact patient care. Here is a situation where management needed to become involved. Had someone been more assertive, this situation could have been resolved sooner. After an investigation, some employees were written up, put on a performance improvement plan (PIP), or were terminated.

## The Rumor Mill

Every job has a mix of people who are pleasant and helpful to work with and people who spread rumors and are chronic liars. And there are those who will be nice to your face but find pleasure in stabbing you in the back. Rumor mongers and liars will stop at nothing to make you look bad or take any opportunity to throw you under the bus. However, there is one question to ask before confronting such a coworker: Is the information you heard from a third party accurate or true? You may have built your assertiveness skills to the point where confronting people in a respectful way is now second nature to you. But this can become a problem if the information you received is only partly true or not true at all. Now you have two problems: the original issue you attempted to rectify and a second issue from which you may wind up backpedaling or apologizing. The effort you made to stand up for yourself now becomes a situation that never should have happened in the first place. So think before you act and do some investigating into what you've been told. It may prevent a minor problem from becoming a much larger one.

## Narcissistic and Rude People

The colleague who blatantly enters a conversation uninvited can range from being annoying to causing confusion and frustration in the workplace. These people intrude on meetings, break into your discussions, burst into your office uninvited, and pester you while you are on the phone. They are basically narcissists who believe that what they have to say is more important than what others have to say. They have no compunction about hijacking a conversation and making themselves the focus of the interaction. Often, they are not even aware they are being rude and will cause people to hide when they are spotted coming their way. It will take a person skilled at being assertive to put the rude person in their place. Therapy can help develop these skills.

## Stubborn People

These are people who do not listen very well, are stuck in their own beliefs, and who fear even the slightest bit of change. These stubborn folks engage in selective hearing, are highly obstinate, and may lead one to wonder if there isn't an invisible "wall" blocking messages from sinking in. They may lead you to question your own methods of communication and cause doubt that the message is being sent effectively. Even in a one-to-one situation, someone who is actively choosing not to grasp a simple concept can cause, at minimum, frustration, which can lead to outright anger. These folks avert change and rely on old patterns of behavior to get by. This becomes a problem when a new technology is installed or a new management team takes over and stubborn people cannot make the adjustment. In therapy, communication and assertive skills can be strengthened, but if someone willingly chooses to not adapt (and they are not cognitively impaired), the process of disciplinary action may need to be implemented.

*Retaliatory Behavior*

Unfortunately, there are times where you will come across those who feel powerless and will stoop to sabotaging others' work as a way to get back at them for some perceived slight. They will plan to discredit or actually withhold information that needs to be passed along so that others cannot effectively do their work. Years ago I heard about a problem in a hospital lab where test results were slow to come out. As it turned out, a staff member who was angry at a coworker had decided to retaliate by holding back on their part of the testing in an effort to slow the work and make the coworker look lazy. It was later discovered that certain work was being put aside and then later put back into the "line," which caused confusion and delayed the results. The person who sabotaged the other person's work used control as a way to get back at the other person who'd reportedly slighted him. Not thinking it through, the person who withheld the work was actually delaying the test results from getting back to the doctors, who needed accurate information in a timely manner to know how to treat their patients. Imagine waiting to know if you had cancer, diabetes, or some other serious condition only to have the test results delayed because a couple staff members didn't like each other. Needless to say, after this was discovered, the staff person was fired and the rest of the team was put on notice regarding future behavior.

*Chronic Complainers*

Everyone complains, but some people take complaining to a whole other level, griping about anything and trying to get you to see their point of view no matter how skewed it may be. They complain when they come into work in the morning, at lunchtime, and at the end of the day. And they start up again the next day. It makes you wonder that if they are so unhappy, maybe they should take responsibility and make some changes in their lives. But they probably won't and will continue to make your life miserable. Complainers are not happy people and can be annoying by making the work environment an uncomfortable place to be in. These are people who perpetuate problems without coming up with solutions. You may need to develop your own coping strategies to tune out the repetitive whining of these unhappy individuals.

*Gossipers*

People who gossip, like rumor mongers, are another group of people who like the control of having information they believe others don't have but want. They are the "gatekeepers" of their precious information and will disseminate it at a time and in a way that gets them the most enjoyment. They can also control the degree of accuracy of the information or change it entirely. As we discussed with those who tend to undermine others, it is important to check the facts before passing the information along. Most people will not do their own investigating and just say, "So and so told me . . ." or "I heard . . ." to try to deflect ownership if the information turns out not to be true. It's human nature to enjoy a juicy bit of gossip every now and again, but some people like to spread rumors as a kind of game. Unfortunately, false rumors can wind up disparaging the innocent. We can decide not to spread gossip and rumors just as we would like others to do for us. It comes down to self-control in whether we want to perpetuate a rumor or be mature enough to stop it.

*Procrastinators*

People who procrastinate and vacillate in their work can carry with them varying amounts of anxiety or may struggle with obsessive compulsive disorder (ocd). These "perfectionists" can never seem to complete a project or get much work done because they are always thinking about or "tweaking" their work. Some procrastinators may actually be able to get a good start on their tasks but get stuck in the end because they believe it can always be better. This is frustrating to employers who have to be on the backs of these folks to get work done and extremely annoying to a team of coworkers relying on everyone to get their part of a project completed.

The anxiety that builds in a procrastinator can be tremendous. I once managed a staff member who had difficulty getting out of his own way at times and had a lot of trouble completing even the smallest of tasks due to his OCD. When this particular staff member decided to leave his position, I politely asked him to clean his office of the stacks upon stacks of papers he had accumulated so the next staff member could come into a clean office. I first asked about a month before he was scheduled to leave, then weeks before, and then during the final week. I went into his office the day before he was leaving, and when I asked why he hadn't cleaned out his office, he claimed he didn't have the time. I spent the following week cleaning out the office, finding papers from ten years prior that had absolutely no value. He just couldn't part with removing even one scrap of paper. To get the office in shape for the new staff member, I went in, rolled up my sleeves, and threw out what amounted to ten shredder loads of useless paper. I don't think the outgoing employee did this out of spite; he was leaving of his own accord. I just think he couldn't bear to throw these items away.

## The Benefit of the Doubt

Working with difficult people can be annoying, frustrating, anger producing, unproductive, and even scary when we face unpredictable behavior. When working with difficult people, the first place to begin an assessment is with yourself. Are you overreacting? Did someone inadvertently hit a "hot button" from some past trauma? Are you overly stressed? Are you overly sensitive? Or is the behavior of the difficult person so blatant you can clearly see where the problem is coming from? Some situations can be worked through with a nonblaming, nonchallenging conversation with the problematic coworker. Perhaps they are stressed due to a loved one with a serious medical issue or an adolescent with a drug addiction, or maybe their marriage is on the rocks. If you are close to your coworker, you may already know what is going on, but in many cases, you won't. Be aware that any questions you ask could hit a sensitive spot in your coworker, and they may be unwilling to discuss their issues. That is their prerogative. However, if coworkers are acting in a way that negatively impacts your ability to do your work, or if sides have been drawn and employees are behaving in a threatening manner, this must be reported to management.

---

Some individuals cannot approach a coworker to tell them how they are feeling. They may feel uneasy with confrontation and uncomfortable about going to the boss. This would be the time to call a therapist for assertiveness training. I have helped quite a few people develop the skills to either respectfully engage a coworker directly or report the bad behavior to their manager. Not addressing the issue in either fashion can cause continued grief, stress, and a sense of dread in the workplace. Calling a therapist may be overdue, but it will start the process of learning to stand up for yourself in and out of the workplace.

# Chapter 10

---

# Assertiveness Issues

*You Can Say How You Feel*

In the last chapter, we ended with a discussion on the value of assertiveness skills in standing for what you believe is right and being able
to freely speak your mind. As a matter of fact, you will find examples
throughout this book where being assertive produced the best possible outcome. But in order to be assertive, you have to begin with
some simple questions that may not have simple answers. For example,
what does assertiveness mean to you? Are you willing to try being
more assertive in particularly difficult situations? Do you understand
that productive, effective assertiveness requires empathy, respect, and
sensitivity for the other person as well as being confident in how you
approach the situation? And perhaps most important, are you willing
to change? As this chapter moves forward, think about these questions
and how they apply to you being happier and more confident in life.
Some information in this chapter is adapted from the book *Assertiveness: A Practical Approach*, by Stephanie Holland and Clare Ward.[15]

### Understanding Assertiveness

So what is assertiveness? Assertiveness can be defined in a number of
ways. You may think you need tons of confidence to be assertive. Confidence is helpful, but you don't need to let a lack of confidence hold

you back from starting to be assertive. Just starting lets you practice, and the more we practice something, in this case assertiveness, the more our confidence grows. This is true for just about anything we do. A novice pitcher in the minor leagues must practice his pitching style in order to be confident and make it to the big leagues. A news reporter has to learn how to gather the facts and think on their feet in order to report a breaking news story. And an actor has to not only remember their lines but how to act the part in a movie or a play. We could name example after example of how seasoned professionals had to learn, practice, and then apply confidence in their chosen professions. Learning how to be assertive and then gaining confidence is no different than with the above examples. It can be a little scary, but the only way to learn is to do.

In *Assertiveness: A Practical Approach*, assertiveness is defined in four ways:

1.  The ability to express your ideas and feelings, both positive and negative, in an open, direct and honest manner

2.  The ability to stand up for your rights while respecting the rights of others

3.  The ability to take responsibility for yourself and your actions without judging or blaming other people

4.  The ability to find compromise where conflict arises[16]

I will add two more:

5.  The ability to ask others for small favors

6.  The ability to say no when you really do not want to do something asked of you

Number six can be a problem for a lot of people. How do you say no when asked a favor or given an invitation? Won't you hurt someone's feelings? Won't you appear unsupportive or selfish? Will that person still like you if you say no? And what do you do with the guilt of saying no? That's a lot to think about when someone asks you to do something and you really don't want to. I will present two examples, one when saying no would have saved a lot of grief, another when asking for a favor would have potentially made a situation a lot easier for someone else.

---

For clarification purposes, I am not suggesting that saying "no" is appropriate in all situations. Children and adolescents must go to school, do their homework, and abide by the rules of the home. At work, the chain of command needs to be respected, and projects and workloads of all kinds need to be accomplished in a timely manner. And it would be prudent for couples to have a discussion when they disagree with each other. Saying "no" for the sake of being defiant is not the point here. As adults, weighing options regarding emotional and physical well-being is what saying "no" is all about.

---

## *The Importance of Saying No—Donna*

Donna, who was only marginally interested in NFL football, was offered a ticket to see a local team play on the East Coast—in the middle of December. She was offered this ticket by a new friend she had met at a PTA meeting. The friend, a parent of a child the same age as her own, thought it would be fun if the two of them "bonded" in this fashion. Donna really wasn't into football in the first place, but to be "nice," she accepted the offer. The forecast that day was twenty degrees, with high winds bringing the wind-chill factor to around zero. Because Donna agreed to go, she felt obligated to attend the game with her new friend. As predicted, it was a cold and windy afternoon. Worse, the local team was long removed from further competition that year, and the visiting team was just going through the motions, anticipating the start of the playoffs the following week. For two and a half hours, Donna endured a boring, bitter-cold, and totally unenjoyable day. The entire game she thought, "Why on earth did I agree to this?"

After the game, Donna thanked her friend for the "wonderful" time she had before exiting her friend's car. She thought she would never thaw out. Why did she allow herself to be put in that situation when she knew darn well it would be a terrible time? Was it because she was afraid that if she said no, her friend's feelings would be hurt? Or that her friend would be angry at her or think Donna was ungracious and end their new friendship? Donna was thinking all about her friend and did not give the least amount of thought about herself. The assumption was that Donna would in some way appear an ungrateful person who didn't care about her friend's generosity. The key word here is *assumption*. Did Donna know that all those terrible things would happen if she declined the invitation? Or did she just assume that if the situation were reversed, she would be hurt and angry? If Donna had graciously declined the invitation, all her anxious thoughts, worries, and assumptions would never have developed. After being invited to the game, Donna felt trapped and believed she was in a no-win situation. If she said no, she would feel like a terrible person, and if she said yes, like she did, she would have a miserable afternoon and be viscerally angry at her friend for putting her through all this. Donna believed that the better of the two evils was to put herself in a bad situation rather than risk looking like an unfriendly person. Donna could have saved herself a lot of angst if she had just been honest from the beginning. No one will melt, break, die, or go insane if we say no. You may think they will, but they won't. Just because you think something is going to happen doesn't mean it will. There is no cause and effect here.

A word about guilt—it is a useless emotion that can cause us endless grief. As children we are taught right from wrong by parents or care-givers and when and where to say certain things. It's called being polite and having manners. However, as we mature, we are more inclined to want to "test the waters" in order to express ourselves and our opinions. If you were raised in a home where you were able to express yourself, as you got older, your communication skills would have been honed, and the feedback you would have received would, in all likelihood, be positive. But if you were shut down as a child and raised with the belief that "children are to be seen and not heard," your communication skills would not be well developed and you would be disinclined to share your thoughts. There would be an inherent fear that you could not say anything right and that you would be a bad person if you said something that was not in line with what others thought. If you did venture out into the world with your own opinions and were criticized for it, guilt in the form of shame would manifest, which equals "I must be a bad person." It's healthy to have your own opinion, even if no one else shares it. And it takes skill to put guilt into a "box" or extinguish it if it pops up. We will discuss more of this later.

This second example is also part of being assertive, but it's the flip side of the first. We are allowed to say no, just as others can say no to us. This next example is one of being assertive enough to ask a friend for help with a job that would be far easier with an extra set of hands. I have encountered many people who have told me they would never inconvenience anyone to help them with their "petty" situations, but they have also acknowledged that they would help a friend at a moment's notice. Why wouldn't it be okay to ask someone close to you for a favor when you would help them with whatever they asked?

### It's Okay to Ask for Help—Jim

Jim had a son who was moving into the City after landing a great job with an investment company. Everyone was proud of Jim's son and the fact he would be living on his own, paying his own bills, and being responsible for everyday life in a career for which he'd worked hard. The only issue was that Jim needed to find a way to get his son's furniture from the basement of their home into the new (walk-up) apartment in the City. Of course, Jim's son would be helping, but with Jim's delicate back, he wasn't sure how much help he would be. Jim was not the kind of person to ask anyone for help. He didn't want to "bother" anyone and said he and his son could do the job themselves. Jim's self-esteem had never been very high, and on some level he felt he did not deserve help from others or was worthy enough to ask for help. Jim rented a U-Haul, the two loaded it, and into the City they drove.

Jim and his son outlined a plan on how they would move the furniture. The apartment building was on the third floor of an older structure with a narrow staircase. For hours, Jim and his son pushed, pulled, lifted, twisted, and shoved the furniture up the stairs, often having to realign the furniture to make it fit. Jim thought he was in pretty good shape, but he was admittedly getting tired. With just two more pieces of furniture to go, he and his son could see the light at the end of the tunnel. But suddenly, as Jim was pushing a bookcase up the stairs, it slipped out of his son's hands. Jim grabbed for it in an awkward way and wrenched his neck and back in the process. Jim's son managed to stabilize the bookcase on a step, but his father, now hunched over, could not stand up. Jim's son put the bookcase back into the truck and drove to the nearest emergency room. It was later determined that Jim had torn a shoulder ligament and pulled a lower-back muscle. It would take months to recover, and Jim was unable to engage in his normal activities for the rest of the summer. If Jim had reached out to a friend, perhaps this accident would never have happened. So much for not wanting to bother his friends!

In the two scenarios above, we see examples of how a lack of assertiveness can complicate life. If Donna had only simply said, "No, thank you," she could have saved herself a lot of grief. And Jim might not have been injured if he had only asked a friend to lend him a hand. In both examples we see how a lack of assertiveness made two people very uncomfortable. Lack of assertiveness skills is not only problematic around friends and family but in other areas of our life as well. In the work environment, we need to use assertiveness to help build confidence and competence and to address professional issues as they arise. You may need to be assertive with your family of origin and also your immediate family. Now, remember, being assertive is not being aggressive (we'll discuss aggression a little later in this chapter). Assertiveness is being able to make a reasonable request or ask a favor of another person while respecting their position. As the Rolling Stones said, "You can't always get what you want,"[17] but it's okay to try.

Another area where being assertive is helpful is in questioning a bill or receipt that looks in error. Calling a billing department or bringing a receipt back to a cashier for an explanation is the right thing to do. Being assertive is not being aggressive; it's politely questioning what appears to be an error. Again, some people find it difficult to pick up the phone and question a bill. They may say, "I don't like confrontation." However, if there was a mistake that could put money back in your pocket, isn't it worth the call?

---

As mentioned earlier, I have helped many in my private practice learn to be more assertive in their daily lives. Problems going back to childhood or issues stemming from abuse or an alcoholic home could all be reasons people find it difficult to be assertive. And to ask someone to try to be assertive without having some basic assertiveness skills training can send their anxiety through the roof. Call a therapist if the words on the page speak to you. It's better to get started now than to never get started at all.

---

## Door-Mat Syndrome

Another behavior type is that of passivity, or the "doormat" syndrome. Why doormat? As you have probably guessed, passive people let others walk all over them. They are hesitant speak up, share their opinion, or ask for help, and they would rather remain in the background than join in. This trait is characterized by feelings of powerlessness, low self-esteem, anxiety, and an inability to take control of their lives. Passive people will let others do the talking for them whether the information presented is right or wrong. Those who are passive will never correct another person but get corrected by others frequently. Passive individuals allow others to trample on them and, although hurting, will never put a stop to it. They often will agree with others outwardly but disagree internally. Those who remain passive have an inability to take responsibility for their feelings and will actually bury their true feelings. Change is often difficult for them.

### Speaking Up Could Have Saved Them a Lot of Money— Debra and Bill

Passivity can be traced back to unmet childhood needs or developmental stages that were skipped due to poor parenting, neglect, or outright abuse. I was working with a woman once who talked about her passivity in her marriage. Debra and her husband, Bill, lived a middle-class life. Debra worked in health care, and Bill was always looking for a business opportunity, although several in the past had been unsuccessful. One day, he told Debra he had found a deli business he would like to invest in with partners. He didn't know the partners but was a mutual acquaintance of one of the investors. Although Debra quietly cautioned Bill about the investment because he did not know who he was working with, Bill disregarded Debra's concerns and accused her of trying to quash the deal. Bill wanted to use all of the $100,000 in their savings and explained to Debra that he'd reviewed the business plan and found it to be sound. Debra, as before, felt her input would not be heard, so she kept her thoughts to herself.

Bill bought part of the business and agreed to work there every day, along with another investor; the other two investors would be silent partners. He worked hard to try to make the sales not only to meet the overhead but to make himself and his partners a salary. Business was good, and Bill was working seven days a week. However, after some time, his partner began to take time off, stating that he couldn't work every day. Since the investors' cash flow was tight, they were in no position to hire an employee, and Bill could not work the business alone. Bill called for a meeting with all the partners to discuss the situation. He thought it went well and felt confident that the problem had been resolved. In the meantime, Bill's wife remained silent because she didn't want to get in the way of his "dream" job, but she was secretly worried about the money he had invested. Back at work, Bill realized that the problem was not resolved. His partner continued to call out.

Bill wanted to deliver lunch to the local businesses, but when Bill's partner was out, he could not make deliveries and lost that potential income. A few months later, he was essentially running the deli by himself and realized that without the needed help, the business was beginning to lose equity. Bill worked even harder, but the business kept losing money. After a little over a year, alone and without any help from his partners, Bill realized he would have to go out of business. The business was closed, and the hardware sold at an auction. Debra knew this day was coming as she had experienced Bill's failed business ventures in the past. In the end, Bill lost nearly all of their $100,000 savings, which she and Bill were putting away for their kids' college education. Should Debra have spoken up and insisted Bill not make the investment? Another wife may have, but Debra's passivity and childhood history wouldn't allow her to do so. She later reported that her parents were alcoholics and spent an inordinate amount of time with their friends at house parties and drinking, which left little time for Debra. And like other adult children of alcoholics, the result was that her self-esteem was often low. Perhaps if Debra had made a decision to get into therapy sooner, she could have developed some assertiveness skills, if only to be able to have an adult-to-adult discussion about Bill's shaky investment plans.

*Thwarted Growth—Edward*

Edward is in his early fifties and works in health care. Edward is not a happy person. He has been working in patient transport for over ten years, and each year he says he needs to leave, but he never does. Patient transport doesn't pay all that much, and as Edward has gotten older, he has begun to develop arthritis and other physical ailments that make his job harder. Never having married, he lives a solitary life in a one-bedroom apartment in a blue-collar neighborhood and has no friends. Those who meet Edward would say he is a timid, quiet person.

At work, he does what he is told and appears to do a satisfactory job. As Edward was growing up, he reported his parents never gave him much of a push to get ahead in life. Edward has previously worked jobs he's enjoyed, but at this point in his life, he feels stuck and defeated. This is a person whose passivity is preventing him from making a move to bring more happiness into his life. He is a bright person, which is a strength, but he lacks motivation and drive—two qualities necessary for him to succeed. Edward is convinced that due to his age, no one will hire him, and so he barely tries. And his self-esteem is practically nonexistent. At times, when Edward sees some progress, his mood and energy levels rise. But when the slightest defeat comes along, all is lost. Even though a steady course of therapy would benefit Edward , he has been in and out of treatment over the last several years.

Edward's overly passive personality has precluded him from making any changes in his life. He afraid of taking any risks but will verbalize his displeasure with the status quo. He lives a very uncomfortable life. He is stuck and cannot seem to move in any direction. Here is a case where doing something—anything—could bring about a new perspective for Edward. But his passivity, faulty belief system, and strong anxiety make it difficult for him to generate the strength to move forward.

---

Passivity can prevent a person from expressing themselves, which can be extremely frustrating and anger producing. A passive person often bottles up their feelings because they believe it is "safer" to remain quiet rather than speak up. This is a painful way to go through life. If you are tired of biting your tongue and would like to learn how to express yourself, call a therapist and begin the necessary work to build assertiveness skills one brick at a time. There are therapists who specialize in self-esteem building and assertiveness-skills training. Why wait when you can be liberated from your silent prison?

---

## Aggression

A third behavior type is someone who uses aggression when interacting with others. These people tend to be narcissistic, controlling, intimidating, and poor listeners. They may even believe they are being assertive when, in fact, they are being aggressive. Remember, the distinguishing feature of an assertive person is the ability to stand up for your rights while respecting the rights of others. There is no place for fear and intimidation in assertiveness. We don't need to speak loudly or make it a one-way conversation. An assertive person will, more than likely, use "I" statements to describe how they are feeling, with no intent on blaming (i.e., "I feel angry when you . . ." verses "It's your fault that . . ."). The aggressor also has a strong desire to "win," and any interaction becomes a one-sided argument. Compromise is seen as a loss in the aggressor's eyes. They feel strong interactions signify confidence and a sense of conviction. In reality, the aggressor has very little self-worth and little interest in respecting others.

*Aggressive Behavior Ruined the Day—Steven*

Steven is a bright, prominent professional who has a worldly sense about him. He and his wife, Marie, and their two small children live a comfortable life. On a trip to the West Coast to visit friends, Steven and Marie were having dinner at an outdoor restaurant with the other couple when the food they'd ordered started coming out in an irregular fashion. Steven received his plate, but not the others. Then, after about ten minutes, two more dinners came out, but there was still one person without their food. Ten more minutes went by before the final dinner was served. Because he was "polite" enough to wait until everyone had their food, Steven's dinner was now cold, and he returned it to the kitchen. In the meantime, the rest of the group wondered if they should wait for Steven's food to come back out or start eating. Steven assured them they should start eating so that their food would not get cold. Steven's food arrived shortly thereafter, but it was now overcooked, and he felt it had been microwaved. He sent the meal back a second time.

At this point, Steven was angry. He felt the dinner was ruined. When the waiter came back to the table, Steven let him have it. He reportedly laid into the waiter for all the mistakes the restaurant had made and blamed them not only for ruining the dinner but for getting him so upset. Steven loudly listed everything that had gone wrong from the minute they arrived. His wife and friends were mortified. After Stephen finished berating the restaurant staff, the two couples left in silence.

Stephen and his wife had it out when they went back to their hotel room. Marie was primarily upset over the embarrassment she felt, not only on behalf of their friends but also on behalf of the restaurant staff and other diners. Steven defended his behavior as being chivalrous as he was the one who had taken control of what he thought was unacceptable treatment on the part of the restaurant. Steven's wife acknowledged that the food was not correctly served, but in no way did the wait staff deserve to be attacked so harshly. Needless to say, the couple's vacation from that point forward was not much fun. Later, Marie spoke to the other couple, and, not surprisingly, she found them wondering why Stephen's reaction was so over-the-top. Luckily, Stephen and his wife were returning home the following morning, but this incident bothered Marie for quite some time. Days later, when Steven attempted to justify his behavior again, she indicated that she no longer wanted to discuss the incident. This put a wrinkle in their relationship as they tried to move beyond it. Unfortunately, like Stephen, too many people are stuck in dysfunctional behavior patterns that negatively affect the quality of their lives and relationships. Fortunately, Steven agreed to call a therapist shortly after arriving home to work on his aggressive and angry behavior.

## Passive-Aggressive Behavior

Passive-aggressive people are as angry as those who are outwardly aggressive, but their aggression is held inwardly. These people are both passive (they are unable to assertively let another person know how they really feel) but also aggressive, in that their anger is expressed in a more secret, behind-the-scenes way. Like passive people, passive-aggressive individuals have low self-esteem, but they are actually seething inside and express their anger in nonconfrontational ways.

### Problems with the Boss—Sam

Sam felt humiliated and was embarrassed that his boss had negatively and openly critiqued his portion of a project his team had been working on. Everyone knew Sam could never confront his boss in public or even behind closed doors, and they felt bad he'd been reprimanded in front of everyone. Sam's anger was so great he felt as if he were going to burst. On the way to his car one day, Sam slowly and methodically took his key and put a deep scratch, bumper-to-bumper, in the side of his boss's new car, then quietly got into his car and drove home. The slight guilt he felt over what he'd done was superseded by his anger, and he justified his behavior by blaming his boss for making him feel so bad. Naturally, his boss's disrespectful behavior did not cause Sam to key his car. Sure, Sam's boss often came across as a bully to Sam and others. But the real problem here was Sam's inability to stand up for himself in an assertive way. If Sam had been able to do so, he probably could have requested a meeting with his boss at the end of the day and explained how he felt when his boss yelled at him. Perhaps Sam's boss would have apologized and indicated he was just having a bad day. It's also possible that the boss would have chosen to not hear Sam out or apologized. But without Sam exercising assertiveness, there was zero chance of anything positive occurring.

We cannot predict what will happen if we do speak up, but we can be sure that nothing will transpire if we don't. When we are assertive, we are telling others it's not okay to speak to us without respect, and we let them know how we feel when they do that. To be assertive is to show the world that you think enough of yourself that you won't allow others to disrespect you. Remember the "I" statements? This would have been a good time for Sam to say, "I felt humiliated when you talked to me like that." Or "I feel angry when you say negative things about me." In that case, Sam would be communicating how he feels when something happens without putting the other person, in this case his boss, on the defensive. Passive people believe they are essentially worthless and not worthy of defending. They let others abuse them over and over to the point that their already low self-esteem gets even lower. Eventually, they may not even find anything remotely positive to say about themselves.

## Unable to Confront His Wife—Brian

Most people would agree Brian and Sue have a good marriage. They have two children, see family regularly, and have friends with whom they socialize. Brian would be described as a quiet guy who works as an accountant, while his wife is outgoing and works in an administrative position in a hospital. They have been married for nine years and are settled into their suburban lifestyle. Whatever success the couple has achieved is noticeable, but Brian has confided in friends that he is not particular happy with how his wife speaks to him. Sue continually bosses him around and finds fault with practically everything he does. If Sue tells Brian to do something and he does it "wrong," she disparages him. Brian doesn't remember his wife being so bossy when they first met and defends her by telling others that she has become more and more stressed out due to excessive job demands. Nevertheless, he also complains he is getting tired of being bullied by his wife, but because he is so passive, he is afraid to confront her.

This is where Brian's passive-aggressive behavior starts to emerge. He has started "getting even" with his wife with behind-the-scenes behaviors he knows will annoy her. For example, when Sue was once rushing to get out the door to go to work one day, Brian surreptitiously hid her car keys and enjoyed watching her panic. Brian sometimes hides his wife's jewelry, clothing, and even mail, until those items turn up in odd places. Brian has even gone as far as periodically hiding his wife's monthly car payment statement so that she incurs late fees. All this is due to the fact that Brian cannot muster the courage to be assertive with his domineering wife. He may not openly confront her, but he secretly devises ways to watch her squirm when he throws "curveballs" at her. This may seem like childish behavior, but for people who lack assertiveness skills, this is a level to which they may stoop.

I worked with Brian in trying to develop the assertiveness skills he needed to stand up to his wife, but his attempts to assert himself were always overrun by his wife's controlling behavior. I'm not sure where the couple stands today, and I'm not certain they are still together (something tells me that they are, because it takes a high level of assertiveness and self-confidence for one spouse to tell the other that the marriage is over and it's unlikely that Brian could do that). Unless Brian is able to stand his ground on issues that are important to him, he will continue to be miserable for a long time.

---

We've seen what can happen if a person lacking assertiveness skills is held "hostage" by a controlling person or people who know their "victim" is passive and they can have their way with them. Being passive-aggressive is not the way to live your life. If you find yourself in this position and want to become a stronger person, pick up the phone and call a therapist today. Being assertive is much healthier and more effective. You may rock the boat as you get stronger, but ultimately your self-esteem will grow and you will feel a lot more comfortable in your own skin.

# Chapter 11

# The Complexity of Adolescence

## The Toughest Time of Their Lives

Adolescence is a time of exploration, growth, maturation, and greater awareness of the world. It is a time of change physically, emotionally, intellectually, cognitively, psychologically, and socially. The way the world is seen by an adolescent evolves anywhere from rather simple notions about life to thinking about and solving complex problems. The years of adolescence can also bring confusion, anxiety, depression, body-image issues, substance abuse, repressed feelings, self-doubt, and suicidal thoughts, unless guided properly by a parent or other caregiver. In this chapter we will look at the many challenges adolescents face in addition to their changing behaviors, bodies, and minds.

---

A cautionary note regarding adolescent problems: As the adolescent changes, many of the goals they have set for themselves change too. Maneuvering through the adolescent years is not a linear process, and someone who seems "all grown up" one day may make some serious miscalculations in judgment another day. Also, normal adolescent behaviors such as sleeping late, isolating themselves in their room, and being "moody" can mirror behavior such as substance abuse, even though there is no drug use occurring. As a parent, you wouldn't want to blame your adolescent for using drugs when in fact they are going through a perfectly normal process in becoming an adult. In this chapter, we learn it is up to the parent or caregiver to recognize problem behaviors that may indicate their teen needs help. Teens may not always be able to communicate when they are having problems, so it is up to the adults to be aware of their adolescents' behaviors without being too intrusive.

The adolescent years transport a person from childhood to young adulthood. When does adolescence begin, and when does it end? There have been debates in the past as to the actual age or range of ages that encompasses adolescence, and it has been determined that there are three stages during this period: early adolescence (ages 10–15), middle adolescence (ages 14–18), and late adolescence (ages 17–22). These ages are not written in stone but can be used as a guide during the adolescent's developmental stages.

Each stage brings about its own challenges. There will be situations and decisions over which the adolescent has control, such as who their friends are, what area of study they would like to focus on, what sport they would like to try out for, and how they would like to present themselves in a social context (hairstyles, clothing, etc.). But the adolescent will find that the more serious issues regarding health, learning disabilities, mental-health problems, bullying, abuse in the home, and parental substance abuse or divorce may be out of their control and that little, if anything, can be done. The differentiation between what is in the adolescent's control and what is not can cause anxiety and depression. And if an adolescent grows up in an environment where the parents are drug or alcohol abusers, the child may not be supported as they navigate their normal developmental stages, leaving a gap of uncompleted development that carries into adulthood.

## Anxiety, Depression, and Suicide

The adolescent years can be a roller coaster of emotions. Teens are not only aware of the physical changes they are experiencing but how they view the world and their role in it. It would be prudent for a parent or caregiver to discuss these changes to help normalize what the adolescent may be thinking and feeling. Without this guidance, a teen may be left wondering what is typical and natural in their developmental stage and what is not.

Some signs to look for regarding anxiety and depression are:

- ◉ Irritability
- ◉ Isolative behavior
- ◉ Loss of interest in activities they once liked to do
- ◉ A drop in school grades
- ◉ Increase or decrease in sleep or appetite
- ◉ Difficulty concentrating
- ◉ Feelings of worthlessness or thoughts of suicide and death

These are serious symptoms of anxiety and depression. If left untreated, a major depressive disorder with accompanying symptoms can lead to suicidal ideation or the taking of one's own life. One must never discount a verbal threat of suicide as mere attention-seeking behavior. The threat must be treated in all seriousness, and the adolescent taken immediately to the emergency room. This is the time to get your adolescent into therapy so they can discuss with a professional what may have triggered their negative thoughts. Since mental-health and substance-use disorders frequently accompany suicidal behavior, other high-risk behaviors to look for are:

1. Extreme personality changes
2. Feelings of worthlessness
3. Withdrawal from family and friends

4. Poor hygiene

5. Substance abuse

6. Struggles with sexuality

7. Giving away favorite belongings

8. Getting "affairs" in order

9. Prior suicide attempts

10. Family turmoil

11. Breakup with a boyfriend or girlfriend

12. Major disappointments or rejection

13. Having a close friend or family member commit suicide

---

A "fragile" adolescent who demonstrates any of the above-mentioned behaviors, especially suicidal ideation, *must* be in therapy and *must* see a psychiatrist for possible medication treatment. Here are some additional steps to take: (1) Do not leave the person contemplating suicide alone, (2) do not blame the individual for their "dark" thoughts, (3) if necessary, take the adolescent to the nearest emergency room, (4) if he or she refuses to go, call the police, and (5) support the individual and encourage compliance with treatment. Adolescent suicide is real, and there are often signs that someone is depressed and suicidal. Do not ignore them!

---

## Substance Abuse

Another major problem during adolescence is substance abuse. As the adolescent's world is quickly changing, and they are experiencing and exploring the world differently than when they were young, experimentation in many areas of life may occur, including social drug use. Some signs that may indicate an adolescent is using drugs are major and sudden changes in appearance and behavior, changes noticed at home, and changes observed in school, accompanied with failing grades.

*Signs in the Home*

- Loss of interest in family activities
- Disrespectful toward family members
- Disappearance of money and other valuables
- Lies about friends or activities
- Not coming home on time
- Drug paraphernalia, such as rolling papers, bongs, pipes, and baggies or small plastic wrappers or rubber bands

*Signs in Relation to School*

- Sudden drop in grades
- Loss of interest in learning
- Skipping class or sleeping in class
- Poor attitude toward school authority
- Not getting homework done
- Not informing parents of teachers' meetings, open houses, etc.

*Physical and Emotional Signs*

- Wide mood swings / "hair-triggered" temper tantrums
- Hanging out with new friends
- Drastic weight loss
- Poor hygiene / always looks disheveled
- Always needs money and will lie about what it's used for
- Overly tired / hyperactive or agitated
- Alcohol or drugs on breath

## As Parents or Caregivers, What Do You Do?

◉ Talk with your adolescent about the changes you have noticed.

◉ Support your adolescent but do not play the role of a friend. You are the parent!

◉ Set rules in the home and use "leverage" if necessary (decide to take away your adolescent's computer, cell phone, or car, and do it!).

◉ Do not feel guilty for enforcing the rules.

◉ Model good behavior around your adolescent.

◉ Offer to help the adolescent with detox, rehab, outpatient programs, or AA/NA meetings but be careful not to enable them (give them too much leeway or go against your own rules).

◉ Very important: as much as possible, try to be on the same parenting page as your spouse to avoid confusion and miscommunication.

If your adolescent has reached this point, it is imperative you seek immediate help. Many adolescents will minimize their drug use and try to have you questioning yourself about how bad the situation has become. This is the time to be firm with your adolescent (they don't have a choice in the matter) and point out the many signs in and out of the home you and others have observed. Many teens assert they have control over their drug use but deep down are fearful and aware of how quickly they have become addicted. At this point the adolescent will become desperate and can only think about getting another "hit" and in all likelihood will do just about anything to get one.

The question now becomes "What do I do if my adolescent refuses treatment?" If a parent or caregiver has offered help through detox, rehab, inpatient and outpatient programs with counselors, therapists, and doctors, and the adolescent refuses, the logical and moral question now becomes "Can I stand firm with 'tough love' to help my child, or will I be an enabler or just a bystander in my child's life?" This can be the toughest decision for any parent or caregiver. I have actually heard of a mother who would drive her child into bad neighborhoods to buy drugs because she felt it was "safer" than having him walk there on his own. Is this enabling or love? It's certainly hard to understand. At this point, it would be prudent for the parent or caregiver to be in therapy to discuss the options available to them in their efforts to help their loved one. No one has total control in life, but entering therapy for your own mental health and having the support of a therapist can bring great comfort.

## Peer Pressure

Peer pressure refers to the influence exerted by a social group in encouraging a person to change his or her attitudes, values, or behavior in order to conform to group norms. Peer pressure is influential because adolescents want to be liked, fit in, and perceived as being "chill" or "cool," and accepted as they are. Other adolescents want others to take the lead in helping peers experience something new, and many will view their peers as "family" and will begin to rely on and trust in them, often for something they may not be getting at home. There are two types of peer pressure:

- ◉ A large group such as a school, club, or gang that dictates clothing, music, behaviors, and other trends
- ◉ A small group of just one or several friends that is more "personal" than a larger group.

Having interactions with friends at school or in town in and of itself is healthy in that it teaches the adolescent socialization skills. However, peer pressure to do things that run counter to the beliefs and values in the home may cause conflict, especially if the adolescent is trying to fit in with new friends or a new group. Below is a list of negative peer pressures that can lead to high-risk behaviors:

- ◉ Drinking alcohol, doing drugs, smoking cigarettes
- ◉ Having sex, especially unprotected sex

- ⊚ Gang membership
- ⊚ Criminal activity
- ⊚ Disrespect of authority, including teachers, parents, and law enforcement
- ⊚ Cessation of educational or career goals

Signs that a parent or caregiver may observe if the adolescent is succumbing to peer pressure:

- ⊚ Sudden attitude and personality changes
- ⊚ Secrecy not observed before
- ⊚ Fighting more with siblings and parents
- ⊚ Wearing uncharacteristic clothing with patches or colors never worn before
- ⊚ Getting arrested for shoplifting or other theft
- ⊚ Appearing intoxicated, incoherent, or "high"
- ⊚ Hanging around "new" friends parents or caregivers do not know
- ⊚ Abandonment of activities normally engaged in

The above lists of adolescent high-risk behaviors and signs of giving in to peer pressure are not exhaustive. The key here is to vigilantly watch for sudden changes in your adolescent's demeanor, personality, behavior, and circle of friends that cannot be explained by the normal maturation process.

---

If you notice that your adolescent is beginning to change in ways not characteristic of their normal behavior, now is the time to call a therapist. Getting your adolescent into treatment is imperative when these high-risk behaviors are first noticed; however, it's common for parents to be in "denial" about their adolescent's behavior with the hope that they will "outgrow" these issues and everything will return to normal. This is the time to **step up and be the parent** and to call a therapist. If negative behaviors are observed early on, the adolescent may be more inclined to talk to a therapist, and his or her issues may be easier to resolve. But once certain behaviors become entrenched and peer pressure has led the adolescent down the wrong path, it is much more difficult to have the adolescent comply with your requests. Remember, for all the issues we have been addressing, it's best to tackle problems *sooner* than later.

## Minimizing High-Risk Behaviors

While it is not possible to control another person's behavior (since each person bears responsibility for their own actions), there are practical ways to guide your adolescent toward more positive behavior choices. Some ways to reduce high-risk behaviors include, but are not limited to:

1. Communicate honestly with your adolescent regarding their behaviors and your concerns. Now is not the time to go dancing around issues with grave consequences at stake. Let your adolescent know what you've been observing and that you are there to help them.

2. Help the adolescent understand the consequences of their actions. Most adolescents do not have the ability to fully understand the cause and effect of their decisions. You'll probably hear, "But that's not going to happen to me." As an adult, you have to educate your adolescent that even if they believe nothing will happen to them, bad things can happen.

3. Demonstrate appropriate decision-making behaviors and judgment. Parents have the opportunity to be wonderful role models to their adolescents. If parents and caregivers show their adolescents what appropriate behavior looks like, they can teach

them how to make each decision a thoughtful choice. Parents who fight a lot, make poor decisions, drink or drug themselves, or show disrespect toward each other are modeling the very behavior they don't want to see their adolescent engage in.

4. Teach your adolescent it's okay to say no; though, as we all know, adolescents have great difficulty not going along with the crowd. Teach your adolescent how to make sound decisions with low-risk outcomes. Using sound judgment, the adolescent can learn how to differentiate right from wrong.

5. **Don't be afraid to be the parent!** I have seen countless parents who want to be "friends" with their adolescent, and more times than not, it backfires on them. Smoking pot with your son or daughter doesn't make you the cool parent. It's just a green light for more and more poor decisions down the road.

A few years ago, a woman called me to schedule a therapy appointment. She impressed me from the minute I met her. She came into treatment to talk about the fact that she and her husband saw parenting much differently from each other and it was causing issues in the home. Jennifer's husband, Mark, was very laissez-faire with the kids. He thought giving them a lot of freedom would make then happy. Jennifer's idea of parenting included teaching good manners, setting limits, modeling respectful behavior, being polite, and expecting her teens to listen to her because she was the parent.

For example, she would put together one meal each night, and dinner was always around six o'clock. She didn't want to hear any moaning that the kids didn't like the meal, and she made it clear it would be the only meal that evening. If the kids didn't come to dinner at six, it was put away. Jennifer made it clear she wasn't serving dinner twice (the irony here is that Jennifer's husband would often come to dinner late). There were no cell phones allowed at the dinner table, and the kids were not allowed to take two bites of their food and run to their rooms with their phones. They had to finish their food before leaving the table. It was made clear that if they rushed through their meal to use their phones, they would lose their phone and other devices for several days. And she stuck to her word.

Mark came to a couple sessions with Jennifer, but due to his liberal upbringing, he didn't see anything wrong with his parenting style. Jennifer was frustrated that Mark didn't see the importance of being on the same page as parents. What is important here is that Jennifer set clear rules and boundaries for her adolescents that, if broken or crossed, had consequences. While Mark thought he was being an effective parent, he was actually doing a disservice to his children by robbing them of the expectations that would help them become respectful, civil, disciplined, successful adults.

6. Don't be afraid to set limits. Limits are essential for emotional and physical health, as well as for teaching your adolescent how to successfully navigate life. Adolescents will test the limits and boundaries at home, at school, in the community, and with other authority figures. Adolescents' bodies and minds are a swirling sea of hormones in which they are learning new ways to interact with the world around them. To say that it can be a confusing time is an understatement. In order to harness the thoughts, feelings, and behaviors of the adolescent, guidelines, rules, and limits need to be set in the early adolescent stage. Setting limits for bedtime, what time to be home if they go to a friend's house, when homework should be done, how much time is spent in front of the TV or with a video game (and the content of the games), how much "junk" food and sugar they can eat, and later, with borrowing the car, where are they going and with whom is essential. Even though we live in a liberal society, teaching adolescents healthy habits, to respect authority, and to follow rules is imperative. Rules and limit-setting will change and can be negotiated as the adolescent grows and matures and as they

demonstrate they can handle more and more responsibility, but remember, maturing through adolescence is not a linear proposition. Younger adolescents can show more maturity than older adolescents, and girls usually mature faster than boys. Having a respectful two-way relationship can help mitigate a lot of the issues that arise during adolescence.

Being the parent means just that! You can make and set rules that have clear and consistent consequences if those rules are disregarded or broken. You do not have to be a dictatorial tyrant; different situations call for different actions. Consistency, respect, and fairness is the way to go, and the earlier this is taught, the better it will be for everyone.

## Self-Esteem

Adolescents often deal with a fragile sense of self-esteem. With so many changes occurring physically, cognitively, and emotionally, their sense of self can be put through the ringer. The adolescent may feel good one day and be down on themselves the next. Hormonal changes, growth, maturation, and pressures at school, home, and with peers can all affect how the adolescent views themselves. Developing confidence and learning to recognize their value requires support from parents and caregivers in three main areas: (1) providing acceptance and affirmation, (2) fostering independence and autonomy, and (3) helping adolescents feel confident and competent.

*Providing Acceptance and Affirmation*

When you provide acceptance and affirmation to your adolescent, you are essentially being positive about their worth, while correcting their behavior. This balance does not condone bad behavior, it helps reinforce good behavior. It is also important to be physically present for the adolescent without smothering them. You don't want to be a "helicopter" parent. You also want to be emotionally present for your adolescent, where you both can share your feelings on various topics, some of which may be uncomfortable for you and your teen. You want to validate your adolescent's feelings and then move on to discuss options for problem-solving. Being an attentive listener is healthy in any relationship, but it's especially important with your adolescent. Teens who feel they are not being heard may believe they are not worth listening to, which can further damage their self-esteem.

*Fostering Independence and Autonomy*

As a parent or caregiver, you want to foster independence and autonomy by encouraging and allowing your adolescent to make many of their own decisions about their life. In the process of fostering autonomy, you want to help your teen develop problem-solving skills so they can begin to figure out options that will help bring about solutions to various issues that may develop. Setting guidelines and principles to help structure your teen's decision-making will help strengthen their self-esteem and build confidence. It is also important to include your adolescent when setting rules around the house. Setting limits and making rules in a dictatorial fashion will only breed resentment and anger and may lead to negative interactions between you and your child. If your child is part of the process of setting fair guidelines, they will be more apt to follow the rules they've taken part in establishing.

An essential component of nurturing your adolescent's independence and autonomy is to respect their physical and emotional space. Part of adolescent maturation is their discovery of how they are changing physically, emotionally, and cognitively. Adolescents need time to themselves to think about the changes they are going through, to process what it means to be maturing, and to try to understand any new feelings they may be experiencing. If you have developed a respectful relationship with your child, they will be more inclined to come to you with questions about changes they may not fully understand.

## Developing Confidence

Adolescents often feel insecure about how they look and bemoan their periodic awkwardness and shyness when talking to the opposite sex. Your teen may have doubts about their physical appearance and may worry about what other people think of them. This can lead your teen to not thinking very highly of themselves. Most of us have successfully navigated the adolescent years. Part of building their self-esteem is guiding them through the same process by helping them develop a sense of confidence and competency.

A great way to do this is by using words of affirmation when talking to your teen. A good coach will not only give a pat on the back and say "great job" when there is success, but that same coach is also there be there to say "You'll get it next time" when someone is not successful. Affirmations are positive statements that help boost your adolescent's self-esteem and help them feel good about themselves. Harsh and demeaning words do the opposite—they make you teen feel bad and worthless. No parent is perfect, and an occasional moment of frustration will not harm your teen, but a daily barrage of harsh or demeaning words will take its toll, not only lowering your adolescent's self-esteem but also breeding resentment and anger.

Another way to help foster confidence in your teen is to acknowledge their worth despite their negative behavior. When your teen is acting out, it is easy to focus only on what they did wrong. This leaves your adolescent feeling bad about themselves and may send a signal that you don't love them. Teens are very sensitive about how others talk to them. Letting your teen know you love them despite their behavior helps them know they are lovable, even when they mess up. It is also important to not push your teen into doing something they don't want to do. For example, forcing your adolescent to try out for sport or a club they really do not want to be a part of will make them approach it halfheartedly, resulting in a subpar performance that can damage self-esteem. A discussion about joining a club or trying out for a sport is fine as long as your teen wants to do it. Then, if they do not make the team, it will not be because of resentment and anger, and your coaching line "You'll get it next time" will help soothe the hurt.

---

If you feel your teen lacks confidence, has a great deal of anxiety, is overly passive and "careful" about everything they say and do, and is not living up to what you believe is their potential, now is the time to call a therapist. Some teens are more assertive than others, and some are outright aggressive or overly passive. A knowledgeable therapist can teach assertiveness skills to your teen and explore the areas surrounding issues concerning self-esteem.

---

## Teen Violence

Most teens are exposed to (and in some cases participate in) a wide range of violence. Peer pressure can be the impetus for a "good" teen to want to fit in with the crowd and go along with certain activities they would not normally participate in. Some adolescents can be drawn into bad situations without knowing the consequences of their actions beforehand. Below are areas a teen will want to avoid, whether they the potential aggressor or victim. Should they become caught up in any of these situations, they need to know they can bring their problems to a parent, caregiver, teacher, or other authority figure for help in knowing what the next steps should be.

### Drugs and Associated Criminal Activity

In addition to psychological, mental, and emotional damage, drugs put an adolescent at risk because they cause impaired thinking and a lack of in judgment (see chapter 8 on substance abuse). Teens can wind up being the victim if they are seen as an easy "target" for aggressors, such as muggers and gang members. Conversely, a drug-impaired adolescent may become the aggressor and engage in activities when high that they would not think about doing when sober. Using drugs and hanging out with an undesirable crowd can lead a teen deeper into the criminal world than they intend. Using, buying, and selling drugs is illegal, and teens have been suspended or expelled from school, arrested for possession, and completely derailed from a successful future. The bottom line is drugs can be highly addictive and, in many circumstances, can kill you. Teens need to know it's not "safe" to overdose merely because Narcan (opioid reversal drug) is now available. The police, EMTs, and hospitals who administer Narcan have to get to you in time before you die. In 2016, nearly seventy thousand people overdosed and died from heroin and other opioids, many of them teens. What makes you think your teen will not be one of them?

*Gangs*

Much has been written about gangs and how they "groom" potential candidates to join their "family." Adolescents who have no guidance, supervision, or support at home often feel they can find all those qualities in gang membership. They are led to believe they will find individuals who will take care of them, watch their back, and make them feel "special"—something they are not getting at home. Gang members will make promises to potential members that seem too good to be true. Potential members are lured by money, glamor, jewelry, fancy cars, being a part of something big, and feeling important. Those who were once a part of a gang and who've left (not an easy feat) report that very few of the promises made by the other gang members held true. They were often given low-level "jobs" or ordered to commit crimes after being initiated.

Gang members have certain attire, graffiti, colors, and tattoos exclusive to the gang. Anyone with similar items could be seriously injured. Gun, drugs, car theft, robberies, fights, muggings, and homicides are all part of these criminal organizations. Many gangs have connections to the big cartels who deal in large quantities of drugs, with millions of dollars in cash and weapons used to protect their enterprise. As we have seen on the news, drug cartels can be ruthless in their efforts to move their product, and anyone who gets in their way can be killed. When gang members are found guilty of murder, they are sent to prison, where they join up with other gang members. Prison is no different than the streets, and the same gang "rules" must be followed or violence can erupt. Being a part of a gang is filled with violence, illegal activity, rival gang fights, and murder.

*Bullying*

Bullying has moved from the schoolyard to every social media device an adolescent owns. We have all seen tragic news reports of the teen who has taken their own life due to the shame and embarrassment of bullying. There was a time when cruel behavior toward a schoolmate was an isolated event that primarily occurred in and around the school property and at school events. Today, anyone can witness or participate in the bullying broadcast across the internet and social media. Secrets are exposed, rumors are spread, and outright false accusations are written about people, causing immense pain for the victim. Disparaging statements about how someone looks, how much they weigh, and about their sexual orientation are posted on social media. Victims have been filmed without their knowledge, and even sexting that may have been meant for only one person has been discovered spread all over school and beyond. Bullying has become a major concern in our adolescent population as teens are exposed, lied to and about, and shamed, sometimes resulting in suicide. Many teens do not realize how hurtful their comments toward other teens can be until it's too late.

---

Talk to your teen about bullying if you see changes in their behavior, if they are isolating in their room, if your teen is reluctant to go to school, or feigning frequent illnesses. As a parent, you need to reach out to the school administrators immediately for help in resolving this problem, even if your adolescent does not want you to report it. Let school guidance counselors know what is going on, and reach out to a therapist who specializes in adolescent bullying to help your teen navigate through this uncomfortable and often dangerous part of their lives.

---

*Internet Predators*

As adults, we know that not all internet contacts are safe. There are a number of them who are not truthful about whom they claim to be. Internet predators will prey on vulnerable adolescents who are either not aware of the threat or who are looking for new "friends." These predators will troll sites that are popular with teens and present themselves as peers looking to just talk, but in actuality, they may be thirty, forty, or older and looking to take advantage of unsuspecting teens. They will post photos of much younger men to mask their age and as a way to bring credibility to their pitch. Predators often try to gain the confidence of adolescents who may have few friends and may be looking for companionship. Internet predators are smooth-talking individuals who zero in on what the adolescent wants to hear and who send compliments to boost their self-esteem with promises to meet in person one day.

A teen who feels alone and unpopular and who may be isolating could follow the instructions of the predator who, after "grooming" the teen over time, will plan to meet at a later date. These teens are getting the attention they crave, attention they are often not getting within their circle of friends or in their family. At some point, the casual talk turns sexual, and the predator may even ask the adolescent to sext nude photos of themselves. If the teen has had little attention in their social circle or is shy or naïve, they may comply. In other cases, the predator will lure teens to a secluded place or actually ask to come over the teen's house when their parents are not home.

A few years ago, Chris Hansen, a journalist with *Dateline NBC*, hosted an episode called *To Catch a Predator*,[18] in which he and his crew posed online as teen girls to see if they could attract predators. They were surprised when they attracted quite a few. After they'd become "acquainted" on line, the predators asked if they could come over to the "teens'" homes to meet.

The show was actually a sting operation coordinated with the police to catch the predators red-handed as they drove to where the teens lived. One by one, the predators were caught on camera making small talk with the teen, and that's when Chris Hansen revealed that they were on *Dateline*. Some of the men started crying, some tried to talk their way out of it, and others attempted to make a run for it. They did not get far as the police were waiting outside. Some of the predators actually started to talk about their "problem" and wanting help. Others proclaimed it was all a misunderstanding. The predators came from all backgrounds—white-collar, blue-collar, schoolteachers, and "model citizens," and most were married with children the same age as their intended victims. The bottom line is this: if you are a parent, be the parent and monitor your teen's internet friends, especially if they do not seem to have any friends at school or in your neighborhood. A teen with no friends who isolates with a computer is "talking" to someone. It's better to have your adolescent mad at you than have them fall prey to an internet creep!

---

If you discover your adolescent is having what you think is an inappropriate relationship online, shut it down and get them into therapy right away. This is not likely something your teen will share with you, so you'll have to be aware and proactive to help your teen stay safe.

---

*Date Rape*

Imagine a girl or woman going out on a date with someone they have gotten to know from school, work, or online and who they have been charmed into believing might turn out to be someone special in their lives. Most dating relationships turn out to be perfectly fine. But what about the date that has nefarious plans for the evening?

The following is a real-life scenario of a date gone horribly wrong. Everything seemed to be going well. The restaurant was beautiful, the food was delicious, and the couple stared into each other's eyes as the night passed on. At some point, the dinner ended, but the couple mutually agreed they were not ready to go home yet. The guy's residence was only a short distance away, and he invited his date to his place for more conversation. She agreed and the stage was set. He ostensibly went into the kitchen to get some drinks, but he had a more sinister plan in mind. He poured the drinks but also put a drug in the glass that would make his date vulnerable and oblivious to his advances. Rohypnol, or "roofies" (there are other drugs that can be used), is a colorless, odorless drug that is undetectable when put into a drink. Shortly after the drink was "dosed," the girl began to feel confused, dizzy, and disoriented and then passed out. This was when the crime occurred. The guy then had his way with his date, who remembered nothing of what occurred when she awakened in the morning. She felt groggy and confused and wanted to know why she was waking up in an unknown environment. The perpetrator claimed they were talking and drinking into the night when they agreed to have sex. Afterward, he said, they'd both passed out until the next morning.

The woman tried hard to remember the experience but couldn't, and any evidence of a sexual experience was explained as an agreed upon, mutual decision. In actuality, the woman had been raped because she had not given her consent. It was not until later, after talking to friends, that the woman suspected what had really happened. However, it was difficult to prove because she had taken a shower, and any evidence had been washed away. Tragically, this kind of occurrence happens in the world of dating no matter the age, race, or socioeconomic status. It's a stark reminder for women to get to know their dates before putting themselves in a vulnerable situation.

---

If you suspect you or your adolescent has been taken advantage of in this way, report it to authorities immediately! Also, your teen should get a gynecological checkup for STDs right away. It's not your teen's fault if they have been taken advantage of, but it's important to take the next step and call a therapist to help process the trauma.

---

*Violence on TV, on the Internet, and in Video Games*

Although statistics fluctuate, it has been calculated that by the age of twelve, the average child has witnessed over eight thousand murders on TV, the internet, and in video games.[19] The evening news is filled with reports of school shootings, war, terrorism at home and abroad, gang violence, and the killings associated with battling drug cartels. There seems to be a constant flow of breaking news that keeps the viewer ever so vigilant. Being an adolescent in the "digital age" has advantages many of us never dreamed of, especially with access to information at lightning speed. But the downside is that some of this information can lead to aggression, bullying, copycat mass shootings, and a desensitization and minimizing of the gravity of such events. Too often on TV we hear about abductions, homicides, suicides, and shootings at schools, concerts, churches, and anywhere large groups of people gather. Drug dealing and gangs, which were once a subculture, are now paraded openly and indiscriminately.

It appears society as a whole has become more thoughtless and brazen. With the internet, we can access all kinds of data for research and academia, conduct our shopping and the click of a button, and acquire knowledge on just about any topic that interests us. The downside, however, are cyberbullies, hackers, violent videos of every kind, pornography, and the "dark web," where criminal activity occurs twenty-four hours a day. Studies have shown that violent and hateful music lyrics raise aggression in adolescents. Violent video games have been referred to as "murder simulators" by military professionals in that an individual can imitate real life killing. Insufficient teen supervision, peer pressure, and undiagnosed mental illness, separately or combined, can also contribute to youth violence. Violent tendencies do not just go away on their own. Too often they escalate to the point where the legal system and law enforcement get involved or violent events occur.

---

If your teen is the victim of violence, get the school involved, as well as law enforcement, if necessary. Those bullied should get into therapy immediately to discuss any issues surrounding the embarrassment and shame bullying can cause and the effects, such as low self-esteem and self-doubt, that can plague a troubled teen. If a teen feels trapped and unable to tolerate the abuse any longer, suicide may seem like the only way out.

---

### Grief and Loss

When a parent, sibling, friend, or relative dies, a teen can feel an overwhelming sadness they often need help navigating. They've lost someone who has played an important role in shaping their fragile identity. The feelings generated from the loss can become part of the teen's life forever. As a parent or caregiver, it is important to be available to your adolescent at this time to give support, to talk, and to listen to what they have to say and to try to answer their questions as sensitively and honestly as possible. The adolescent years are confusing enough, and when this type of loss occurs, it can be, for many, a traumatizing event. It's often difficult to know what to say to a teen when the death of a loved one occurs, but listed below are a few statements that have been shown *not* to be helpful to the grieving teen:

◎ "You have to be strong now that your dad is gone."

◎ "It's your job to take care of the family now."

◎ "At least she died quickly and didn't suffer."

◎ "Grandma is happy and in a 'better' place now."

◎ "Don't let others see how sad you are."

Talking about a loved one in an honest way and allowing your teen to express their emotions in a way that is congruent with how they are actually feeling will dispel any notion that your teen is doing something "wrong" in this kind of situation. There is truly no right or wrong way of experiencing a loss such as death. Everyone grieves differently. Oftentimes parents will blend reality with fantasy to buffer the experience. This is not "wrong" per se, and how you speak to your teen may be based on their level of maturity. One's faith may also play a significant role in what they believe about death and dying. The death of a loved one is difficult for everyone, but it is important to note that it can be especially hard on a teen who may feel afraid and confused by the event. Some signs that your teen may need help coping with a death include:

◎ Symptoms of chronic depression

◎ Sleeping problems or restlessness

◎ Academic failure or apathy toward school-related activities

◎ Deterioration of relationships with family or friends

◎ Prolonged isolation from others

◎ Risk-taking behaviors, such as drug or alcohol abuse

◎ Acting overly strong or mature and denying their feelings

◎ Other behaviors that are out of character for your teen

It is often difficult to assess how your adolescent is coping with the loss of a loved one. They may try to be strong and hold their emotions in, thinking that if they seem to be doing well, the rest of the family will not have to worry about them. Other adolescents may act out in anger at home or at school in an attempt to mask the hurt. Your adolescent may experience somatic complaints such as stomach issues, headaches, or other bodily aches and pains. They may even feel they are dying if they experience anxiety attacks they can't explain. If a loved one is terminally ill, that would be the time to call a therapist for your adolescent so that they can express their feelings about the inevitable fate of their family member or friend. If a death occurs suddenly, it would be prudent to call a therapist immediately so that the event can be processed in a professional way.

Chapter 12

# Abuse and Neglect
## The "Hidden" Problem

Sadly, abuse and neglect occur throughout the life cycle, whether in childhood, adolescence, adulthood, and with the elderly, and come in many different forms. Abuse and neglect occur with vulnerable and passive individuals, such as children or adolescents who either don't want to "cause trouble" or think they are going to get someone else in trouble. Other individuals are embarrassed or ashamed that abuse is happening in their own home, such as with a spouse or partner. Elders may not want to report abuse or neglect for fear they will be "punished" with more abuse and neglect.

Although the above-mentioned populations differ in age and circumstance, abuse and neglect can produce the same fear and hurt in everyone. Areas of abuse range from verbal to physical, to sexual, emotional, psychological, and financial. It is most often perpetrated by individuals in a position of power over someone who is in a vulnerable position. Neglect can be just as harmful, but it is not a lashing out—it's a withholding of tasks another person needs help with, such as personal hygiene or the preparation of food. In any case, abuse and neglect can cause great harm to those not in a position to stand up for themselves. Below I will outline the populations abused in three separate sections, beginning with children and adolescents, then adults, and then the elderly. Regardless of age, abuse and neglect are crimes not only in the legal sense but also morally, according to the values we as a society and culture hold dear.

---

I would like to say a few words about abuse and neglect right from the beginning. I believe that as a society it is our responsibility, and for a health-care professional an obligation, to help protect the vulnerable populations we encounter. If a child or adolescent is experiencing abuse, Child Protective Services should be called. If you suspect that an elderly individual is being abused or neglected, a call to Adult Protective Services is in order. These are the two most vulnerable populations because in nearly all instances, they cannot make the call themselves. In the case of adult domestic violence, there are shelters for battered spouses where they can be protected with anonymity. In the case of a young adult, they have to make a decision to leave the abusive environment and seek help through health-care professionals who run community shelters, or find a place to stay with either friends or family. However, the main focus here is to get the abused or neglected help immediately. The work of the therapist comes after the abused person is in a safe environment.

---

## Child and Adolescent Abuse

You see a child who is dirty, scared, and alone. What do you do? Do you ignore the situation? Try to talk to the parents or caregivers? Call the authorities? The decision to get involved in other people's issues is not an easy one given the thought of possible repercussions between neighbors, friends, or even within one's family. It is easier to do nothing, especially if there is fear that a parent or caregiver will be mistakenly blamed for abuse or neglect and will now be investigated by Child Protective Services. Often people will minimize what they see or tell themselves that there must be an explanation for what they are witnessing.

Health-care professionals are obligated to place a call to authorities, even if there is only a suspicion of child abuse. Child Protective Services will go to the home to verify or refute the claim. If nothing is uncovered, the agency professionals will not open a case. If evidence of abuse is discovered, further action will be taken. An anonymous call can be made to Child Protective Services, who will do an assessment and investigate the claim. It is good to know that the life and well-being of a child or adolescent can be saved with just one call.

Child abuse can occur in any culture, race, or ethnic group and can be in the form of physical, emotional, verbal, or sexual abuse. Neglect, which is also a form of abuse, is willfully withholding the basic necessities of life, such as food, clothing, or shelter, from someone who cannot care for themselves. Any form of abuse or neglect can lead to serious injury and possibly even death.

There are a number of signs or symptoms to look for if you suspect a child or adolescent has been abused. Remember, you cannot always rely on the child for answers as they may believe the abuse was their fault or they may want to prevent a loved one from getting into trouble.

◉ Physical abuse involves the nonaccidental harming of a child (i.e., kicking, beating, burning, breaking bones) that cannot be explained away to others or may be lied about. New bruising or bruises that appear to be healing can also show a pattern of abuse.

◉ Verbal abuse comes in the form of belittling, degrading, shaming, or threatening a child. Symptoms can be low self-confidence, social withdrawal, and depression.

◉ Emotional abuse may be manifested by continually making promises to a child only to not come through on those promises or blaming a child for something they may not have done but not giving them the chance to tell their side of the story. Also, pushing a child away when they ask for help or withholding affection can emotionally damage a child. Symptoms include isolating behavior, delayed emotional development, and a heightened need for approval or validation.

◉ Sexual abuse is the violation and forced participation of a child by an adult by touching their breasts or genitals, exposing one's genitals to a child, showing child pornography, having them perform oral sex, or having sexual intercourse with a child. Signs or symptoms include bedwetting, genital or anal bleeding, nightmares, and extreme sexual behavior that seems inappropriate for the child's age.

People often find it hard to understand how anyone can abuse or neglect children and adolescents. In our society, children and adolescents are supposed to be looked after, nurtured, educated, nourished, and supported until they are able to care for themselves. However, sadly, this is not always the case. The following list includes reasons why abuse and neglect occur in the home:

◉ *Substance abuse by parents or caregivers.* In some cases, those in charge of looking after their children are so wrapped up in their drug use that the child is seen as "getting in the way" of their activities and they are neglected because the parents are impaired and are unable to provide care.

◉ *Parents who were abused when they were young.* Often, abuse and neglect becomes a generational problem in which these behaviors are "taught" in the home and are seen as "normal." Children and adolescents who are abused and neglected may, in fact, abuse their children. It isn't until someone breaks the cycle of abuse that it finally ends.

◉ *Young, single, or nonbiological parents.* Cases of abuse may occur in couples living together with children born from a nonbiological parent and who are not seen as the parent's own child. These children may be perceived as someone who doesn't "belong" in the new family. The child may not be treated the same way a biological child would be treated.

◉ *Single parents under stress.* Parents who find themselves alone in their parenting can abuse their children because they are under stress. Many single parents find themselves needing to work several jobs in order to make enough money to pay the bills and put food on the table. This added stress can produce a home where frustration and anger is taken out on the child or adolescent in an effort to maintain a sense of stability and control in the home environment.

◉ *Parental or caregiver mental illness.* In many situations, a parent or caregiver may suffer from a mental illness in which their emotional instability is taken out on the child. Parents' or caregivers' mental illness can be so profound they cannot even take care of themselves, let alone their children. Often, these parents or caregivers find themselves in and out of psychiatric hospitals for mental-health treatment, leaving the child or adolescent in less-than-favorable living conditions while they are out of the home.

◉ *Children with disabilities may increase the burden of the caregiver.* A child with a disability can be a challenge for any household, but it can be especially difficult in a single parent home where stress is all-encompassing. Without a break, a single parent may not always be able to control their emotions when dealing with incessant caregiving responsibilities.

The above list is certainly not all inclusive, but it illustrates some of the reasons why abuse and neglect occur in our society. Children who are abused or neglected suffer not only physically but emotionally. An abused child or adolescent may become withdrawn, depressed and suicidal, or engage in substance abuse in order to escape their pain.

### Domestic Violence

Whether it's called domestic violence; domestic abuse; spousal abuse; or wife, husband, partner battering or stalking, the acting out in anger of one individual toward someone they are or were married to or are or were cohabiting with is a growing problem in American society.

Aggression, humiliation, physical assault, sexual violence, controlling behavior, unpredictable mood swings, the alienation of friends or family, and blame and manipulation all constitute domestic abuse. According to the National Coalition Against Domestic Violence (NCADV) in the United states, an average of twenty people experience intimate partner physical violence every minute.[20] This equates to more than 10 million abuse victims annually. On average, one in four women and one in nine men experience severe intimate-partner physical abuse, intimate-partner sexual violence, and/or intimate-partner stalking. This often leads to fearfulness, severe injury, post-traumatic stress disorder, contraction of sexually transmitted diseases, and, in some cases, death. On a typical day, domestic-violence hotlines nationwide receive over twenty thousand calls. An abuser's access to a firearm increases the risk of intimate-partner homicide by 400 percent. The use of alcohol or other drugs often exacerbates the violence. Domestic violence is prevalent in every community and affects all people regardless of age, socioeconomic status, sexual orientation, gender, race, religion, or nationality. Physical violence is often accompanied by emotionally abusive and controlling behavior that is part of a much larger, systematic pattern of dominance and control.

*Contributing Factors*

Eight out of ten domestic-violence shelters report that more and more women are seeking help; however, with reduced funding, services, and prevention for these shelters, 74 percent of abused women remain in the violent environment longer.[21] With this type of abuse, it is often generational, psychological, and behavioral issues within the abuser that perpetuate the problem. Financial problems within the home are another factor that adds to the incidence domestic violence. Often one spouse works outside the home while the other stays home to take care of the children. In an abusive situation, the working spouse can abuse the other by withholding money or only giving a marginal amount for basic necessities. In some cases, the working spouse lives in and out of the house and may not be home for days or even weeks at a time. One spouse may develop a substance-abuse problem, and all earnings go toward feeding the addiction. In other cases, the spouse who earns the money will permanently leave the family to fend for themselves. The spouse left behind may eventually end up relying on government-assistance.

Although many theories abound concerning domestic violence, I will present two emotional dynamics that give some perspective on this problem.

## Theories of Abuse

1. One theory referred to as the "critical inner voice" is a well-integrated pattern of destructive thoughts toward others and even one's self. The thoughts that make up an internal dialogue are at the root of self-destructive and maladaptive behavior, including domestic abuse. These negative thoughts can undermine any positive thoughts one has about others or themselves, fostering distrust, anger, and delusional beliefs. These inner thoughts usually come from early life experiences that are internalized and taken in as ways to think about oneself and others. Often, many of these thoughts or negative "voices" come from experiences witnessed as a child from a parent, caregiver, or other influential person. These critical inner thoughts can be so overpowering they cause a person to make unhealthy decisions in a matter of seconds. Most people who lash out toward others are unaware that their behaviors are just the tip of the iceberg and a mere fragment of a larger and more pervasive problem.[22]

2. The other theory involves a harmful illusion of connection between a couple that has been referred to as a "fantasy bond." This dynamic feeds into a sense that another person can make you whole and is responsible for your happiness. It's an illusion of mature love and intimacy. Creating a fantasy bond is a form of self-protection and is developed by replacing the real

relating involved in being in love with a form of just going-through the-motions. The degree of reliance on a fantasy bond is proportionate to the degree of frustration and pain experienced in a person's developmental years. If one's parents demonstrated a lack of closeness in their marriage, it is likely that an adult child will demonstrate the same behavior in their relationships. Many people have fears of intimacy and are self-protective yet at the same time are terrified of being alone. Some couples can create an illusion of connection and closeness that allows them to maintain an imagination of love while preserving emotional distance. Ultimately, fantasy bonds greatly reduce the possibility of couples achieving real intimacy.[23]

The above two belief systems can set up an environment of abuse, as illustrated by the "critical voice," which can project negativity, such as mistrust, onto one's partner or a "fantasy bond," in which a couple believes their partner is responsible for their happiness. Whether it's the destructive inner voice of old "tapes" from parents or caregivers playing in the background or expectations that go unfulfilled creating frustration, disappointment, and anger, these dynamics can lead to domestic abuse. Domestic abuse is ultimately about power and control, but, paradoxically, it turns out to be a lack of control from one individual to another.

### Breaking the Cycle

Many who commit abuse were either abused themselves as children or witnessed abuse between family members. In our society, men are taught and expected to be strong, masculine, and more powerful than women, and the "shame" of appearing weak or subservient can trigger some men to become enraged and to act out in violent ways. To break patterns of generational domestic violence, programs need to be implemented that teach offenders ways to recognize certain external triggers so as to be better able to manage impulses internally. Those who are raised in homes where parents or caregivers model respectful behavior toward one another and where feelings can be discussed openly are less likely to become violent later on in life. Habilitation or rehabilitation programs that emphasize self-reflection, self-control, empathy, and responsibility not only toward their partners but toward themselves can help rescue individuals from acting out in destructive ways. Programs that cultivate self-esteem and forgiveness can also help these individuals understand themselves better, putting them in a position of becoming more empathic toward others.

Although there are many factors and dynamics that keep someone in an abusive relationship or going back to one after leaving, no one deserves to experience violence in their home. Many of the abused believe or are made to believe that they are to blame for making their partner angry and that they "deserve" the abuse. Others fear being alone and will withstand and tolerate the violence. Many believe they cannot make it financially on their own or that they need to stay in the relationship for the children. Whatever the reasons, it is important to know that abuse of any kind is not healthy and that there are supportive community programs and shelters. You first want to get to a safe place and receive medical treatment if severely abused. Later, get into counseling in a support group or call an individual therapist or both so that the healing can begin.

## Elder Abuse

Elder abuse is a single or repeated act of violence or lack of appropriate action occurring between an individual and an elder adult that causes harm or distress to that person. It can include people the older person trusts or has a relationship with, such as a spouse, partner, other family members such as adult children, as well as friends or neighbors. It also includes people the older person relies on for services, such as aides within a nursing facility or hospital. Elder abuse can occur because of physical, cognitive, mental health, and financial vulnerability. Like abuse at any age, elder abuse comes down to power and control over someone who does not have the ability to defend themselves.

Below is a list of the types and signs of elder abuse:

⊚ *Physical.* Includes hitting, punching, kicking, burning, pushing, imprisonment or confinement, and withholding medicine and other treatment. Signs include bruising at different stages of healing, scars, and overall poor physical health. Also, rope marks on the wrists may indicate restraint, and broken eyeglasses may have been brought about by a slap or punch.

⊚ *Psychological/emotional.* Humiliation, yelling, name-calling, ridiculing, constant criticizing and blaming. Another form of emotional abuse is nonverbal, such as ignoring, silence, shunning, or withdrawing affection. Signs may include a change in the older adult's personality, social isolation, and a non-responsiveness to questions about care.

⊚ *Financial abuse.* Involves stealing an elder's money or valuables, misappropriation of assets or property, and embezzling of the elder's funds without their knowledge. Look for large withdrawals from the elder's accounts, missing belongings or money, unpaid bills, and unnecessary purchases or services the elder did not make.

⊚ *Sexual abuse.* The forcing of an older adult to take part in any sexual activity without their consent. It is important to state that an elder with dementia many not be able to give or decline consent due to cognitive impairment. Abuse is detected by visible signs on the body, especially around the breasts, genitals, and anus. Additional signs may be torn clothing, bleeding, and frequent infections.

◉ *Neglect.* Deprivation of food, medicine, medical treatment, heat, clothing, comfort, and needed services. Neglect can be active neglect (intentional) or passive neglect (lack of knowledge regarding care), such as leaving a person at risk for falling unattended. Signs include malnutrition, dehydration, poor hygiene, bed sores, medication noncompliance, and deplorable living conditions.

◉ *Abandonment.* Deserting a dependent person with the intent to leave them unattended for a period of time and thereby putting their health or welfare at risk. An older adult may not want to report this due to fear of being abandoned again.

◉ *Rights abuse.* Denying the civil and constitutional rights of a person who is older but not declared mentally incompetent by a court of law. Everyone has basic human rights regardless of age, and an older adult has the right to make decisions for themselves unless declared incompetent by doctors and the courts.

◉ *Institutional abuse.* Physical or psychological abuse, as well as rights violations, in settings where care and assistance is provided to dependent older adults. In the United States, studies have shown a growing rate of abuse in nursing homes, long-term care facilities, and hospitals. Exact statistics are difficult to ascertain as older adults are not always able to report their abuse or may be unreliable historians and report abuse that did not occur. If you believe an older adult is not receiving the proper care or is being abused, the county ombudsman's office should be contacted right away.

Perpetrators of elder abuse can be anyone in a position of trust, control, or authority over the individual. This can be a spouse, partner, relative, friend or neighbor, volunteer worker, paid worker, practitioner, or any other individual with the intent to deprive a vulnerable person of resources. Relatives may also include adult children and their spouses, their offspring, and other extended family members.

What problems can arise in the treatment of the elderly population? In some cases, much older spouses can barely take care of themselves, let alone the sicker spouse, and unintentional neglect can take place. Often the couple's residence can deteriorate to the point where it may need to be condemned by the municipal board of health. And many times a couple may have to be hospitalized just to get them out of conditions of filth and degradation. Sometimes a less-than-mature adult child will ostensibly move in with their parent or parents to help look after them only to use their good graces for a place to live without paying rent. That same adult child may have had a lifetime of troubles and drug abuse and will move into their parents' home only to think about what they can steal to support their drug addiction, all the while neglecting their parents.

There are plenty of con artists out there who prey on elderly who are easily confused and give money, valuables, or sign away real estate to someone they believe is working in their "best interest." Some live-in aides can also manipulate an elder. Since they spend so much time together, the aide may get to know where money or valuables are kept and may physically or emotionally abuse the elder and threaten the withholding of care if they report them.

Institutionally, many staff are not properly trained with the elderly population, others become burned out and just don't care, and others have no regard for the Patients' Bill of Rights. I would like to add that there are many loving and warmhearted individuals who take great care with the elder population. They are patient, taking the time to listen to their patients and understanding that what they are doing is noble and rewarding. Unfortunately, there are those of a criminal mindset who try to use their power and control to take advantage of the older adult. There may also be a diagnosed or undiagnosed history of caregiver mental illness, which can be detrimental to both the caregiver and the elder. A combination of two unwell individuals symbiotically living together can be a recipe for disaster.

Lastly, some older adults may be "groomed" by neighbors or friends who will build trust over time only to surreptitiously help themselves to the elder's money and valuables. As we can see, our elders are a vulnerable population and can easily be taken advantage of, mistreated, and abused, and we should all know what to do if we suspect this activity is taking place.

If you suspect an elder is being abused, call your county Adult Protective Services. They will go to the home and investigate. The call can be made anonymously. If your loved one is in a hospital, subacute rehabilitation center, or long-term care facility, the county ombudsman should be called. The office of the ombudsman will dispatch someone to the facility to investigate the claims reported. You can also call 911 if you believe further abuse is imminent. The abused elder should get medical treatment immediately, and it would be prudent for you to get into therapy if you are a loved one of the abused to discuss your anger, disbelief, and perhaps guilt that you couldn't do more.

Chapter 13

# Existential Angst

*Finding Your Way*

Existential angst not only derives from the human inability to think, feel, and act in the world or experience a love for life but also from the fear of the possibility of nonexistence and/or death. It can be a lonely and isolating place and outright terrifying if one's very existence is in question. Psychologist Carl Jung and philosopher Jean Paul Sartre had similar thoughts about existential angst in that both focused on achieving meaningful existence through development of inner resources, creative exercise of freedom, and overcoming self-deception.[24] In essence, those who experience existential angst feel lost, think they have a purposeless existence, and believe they have been abandoned by life.

Have you ever wondered what life is really all about? Why you are here? What your purpose is? Does your life have meaning? Do you ever ask "Who am I?" These questions have been asked throughout the ages by philosophers, theologians, psychologists, spiritualists, and by others who try to answer these deep questions of life.

Life is full of unanswered questions. And just as with those who fear the "unknown," not knowing the answers to life's most difficult questions can be quite unsettling. Our brain likes complete images and thoughts and will fill in the "gap" if something seems incomplete. If it doesn't have an answer, it will make one up. For people with anxiety, not having a clear and confident answer to life's questions can cause them unpleasant thoughts that are "catastrophizing" in nature. If they don't know what's around the corner, they will "invent" a catastrophic event, which will in all likelihood heighten their anxiety.

As mentioned earlier, mindfulness teaches us to be present in the moment—not in the past, and not the in future. If we can stay focused on the present and an unpleasant event happens, we can do something about it. Many people lament about the past and what they should or shouldn't have done, while others worry about the future and live in a what-if world. Some fear the unknown and bring great anxiety upon themselves when they reflect on how little control they believe they have in their lives. And some people feel helpless and have an absurd idea that others should guide them through their lives and answer the tough questions for them.

I always thought it was interesting how, as humans, we cannot know where we came from and where we will be going, but we have the ability to ask these questions. Other species seem content on just "being," but as humans we are able to ask "Why?" This is where the "angst" comes in for people who feel their lives have no clear meaning and no justified purpose.

In chapter 1, I talked about my own search for meaning and how I felt alone in the process. I knew there had to be more to life than just going through the motions and waiting for something to happen. I have learned that we can wait a long time for significant change to occur. In order for me to create a purposeful existence, I had to face my fears and venture out into the world for meaningful experiences to happen. I remember all those years ago how my therapist explained that when the pain of not changing becomes greater than the change itself, we are able to take a step forward. I have never forgotten those words, for they proved to be true. And I share this often in my private practice.

**What Therapy Can Do**

Therapy is viewed differently by different people. Some come in to "vent" about problems at work or at home or to talk about their less-than-satisfactory marriages and problems with their kids. Some seek help with their anxiety, depression, and other disorders. They also come in to talk about their own or a loved one's addiction, to discuss elderly parent or sibling problems, and many other concrete issues that can bring about quantifiable results. And then there are the issues we have been examining in this chapter—the issues of feeling lost, confused, lacking meaning or purpose in life, and wondering who the person in the mirror is. Not all therapists are qualified or want to even work in this area. Others, like me, feel deep satisfaction in knowing that a client would like to explore the deeper, more spiritual side of life. It's not fun being directionless or feeling that there is no purpose in life, and many opt to immerse themselves in alcohol and drugs to quell the pain or to fill the void in their soul.

### Discovering Our Purpose

Whether life has meaning or purpose and whether we can even get to fully "know" ourselves can be looked at in different ways. In the macro, or larger, sense, the questions we have been exploring comes from age-old thinking on a massive "everything" scale. "Why are we here?" and "What is my purpose in life?" The great existential theorist Victor Frankl once said, "Those who have a 'why' to live can bear with any 'how.'"[25]

For many, these questions are just too incomprehensible to even attempt to answer. However, some try to think of purpose in a micro, or more compact, sense and break the answers into bite-sized pieces. People will report that their purpose in life is to take care of their children. Others find meaning in being a loving wife or husband and maybe a good son or daughter. Some find their purpose through their religion or faith. Teachers find purpose in educating their students. And health-care professionals, such as doctors, social workers, nurses, and others feel they have a calling to help people in need. I know I do. As with other tasks, I believe it is up to each and every one of us to take the responsibility to find a purpose in life. And we need to be introspective enough to look deeply inside ourselves to see who's there.

Someone once asked me what I thought the meaning of life was. I'm not sure why they thought I would have the answer, but after some thought, I came up with, "The meaning of life is to seek out the meaning of life on our individual journeys." Perhaps that doesn't feel satisfying, but I believe it puts a necessary burden on everyone individually, which, in some cases, can make some folks feel alone in this process.

## How Not Knowing Your Purpose Can Cause Anxiety

Taking responsibility for our thinking, behavior, and feelings can raise anxiety for anyone. Not only that, but if we extrapolate our anxieties to the nth degree, we come to most people's greatest fear—death. Let's examine this in a series of questions and answers:

Question: "Who are you?"

Answer: "I don't know"

Question: "What do you fear most about not knowing who you are?"

Answer: "I fear not knowing the person inside me."

Question: "So what if you don't get to know the person inside you?"

Answer: "If I don't know who I am, I may not know what I want in life."

Question: "If you don't know what you want in life, how is that a problem?"

Answer: "If I don't know what I want, how am I supposed to live my life?"

Question: "If you don't know how to live your life, what makes that an issue?"

Answer: "If I don't know how to live my life, I may as well be holed up in my room every day and night doing nothing."

Question: "If you isolated yourself in your room every day and night and did nothing, what would that mean?"

Answer: "I would not be living life and I would die."

So the not knowing, if taken as far as it can go, can mean the fear of death for some. In this case, a person's thoughts and emotions are way out in front of the original question, and it takes some chipping away from question to question to get to how the person really feels. Whether it's unanswered questions about our existence, purpose, or meaning, anxiety and the fear of death can continuously play in the background of someone's mind. This is no way to go through life. Many people struggle with the questions outlined in this chapter, while others are too distracted to even give them much thought. Actually, reality, fear of the unknown, and not knowing our ultimate purpose can get in the way of someone not living up to their potential in life. A therapist can help those with existential angst look at all the value they have that makes life worth living even without having all the answers. Someone may feel that the chocolate ice cream cone they are eating brings meaning and purpose in that moment. Maybe it didn't answer the big mysteries of life, but it was good enough at that time.

I've struggled to find an appropriate place to share my thoughts on how I see the way our lives unfold. I believe this is a good place to share an analogy I've developed about life.

Life is like a pinball machine. Like a pinball, we come hurtling into life, not knowing where we're going or what challenges lie ahead. As our pinball selves, we come in contact with a bumper, which can symbolize a person or event, and go flying in another direction only to hit another bumper-like person or event and go off in yet another direction. Since we cannot predict the future of our pinball selves, every interaction has the potential to send us in a new and *exciting* direction. The point here is we never know who or what will change us, make us switch gears, or push us on a new path, but we should be ready to embrace those changes along the way and recognize that each "bumper" can significantly impact our lives forever.

If you feel depressed and that life has no meaning and are wondering, "Why bother going on?" call 911 or go to your nearest emergency room right away. If you would like to explore some of these "big" questions with a therapist, look for one with whom you can have this discussion. Not every therapist works in this area, so be selective. This can be a rewarding experience and make a meaningful difference in your life.

 # In Conclusion

Over the years, I've worked with many clients on their mental-health issues, and I can say without hesitation that when most people decide to enter therapy, they are coming in too late. People tend to suffer unnecessarily for great lengths of time before they even think about calling a therapist. I did the same thing when I was facing my own struggles. Looking back, I can clearly see how much needless suffering I could have avoided by just picking up the phone and taking that first step. It wasn't something to fear but something that ended up putting me on a path toward a more abundant, happy life. My hope is that you, the reader, will come away with a greater understanding of what constitutes therapy and the therapy process. Now that you are aware of many of the issues keeping people from enjoying a fulfilling, joyful life, hopefully you will come to the realization that there is help and that you do not have to live with the problems holding you back.

In chapter 1 and interspersed throughout the book, I've included some of my real-life struggles as a child, adolescent, and adult. I wanted to let the reader know that reaching out to a therapist for help is not a sign of weakness but of strength in making the necessary changes that lead to more clarity and happiness. For me, it was the turning point in my life. Not only did I get relief from near-debilitating anxiety and depression, I also started to look at some of those "big" questions we discussed in chapter 13. I was as lost and stubborn as they came, but I managed to put many self-defeating thoughts and behaviors aside and took the steps necessary to become a healthier person. I would like to see you do the same.

I have written about what I believe are the most common mental-health and behavioral issues people suffer from today, though, naturally this is not an exhaustive list of mental-health challenges. There are certainly more complex disorders with which people struggle, but the information in this book represents what I have seen in my private practice helping those at work, those who have families and homes to support, students, and a host of others seeking help. Life can be stressful. My hope is that you get into therapy *sooner* than later so that you can move from a black-and-white world into a more colorful one. Below are a few success stories about people who reached out to me for help. My hope is that their successes will encourage you to tackle your struggles with renewed determination and confidence so that you too can live a more abundant life.

## Relationship Renewed

I recently saw a couple for premarital counseling. Although they had dated for several years and then moved in together, there were some nagging issues they wanted to work out before they got married. They reported there were times when they had trouble expressing their feelings to one another. Instead of addressing problems as they came up, they would both suppress their feelings to the point where the next little spat would turn into a major argument. She was the gregarious one, and he was the quiet type. She liked to go to parties to dance and have fun, but he would mostly sit by himself, counting down the minutes to when they would leave. After a short time in therapy, the couple expressed to each other how they both felt about this particular issue. They knew they needed to be more honest and not be afraid to talk about how they felt. By the time they left therapy, they had learned several skills that would improve their communication now and in the future.

*Reunited: Angela and Sean*

Not too long ago I worked with a woman who reported that she and her husband were having marital problems. She was living in the States with her one-year-old child while her husband was deployed halfway around the world in the military. The strain of having him away coupled with all her child-care responsibilities was putting stress on their marriage. It would be six months before he was redeployed to the States, but Angela was not so sure what shape their marriage would be in after Sean came home.

Angela had talked about the fact that she and Sean would find themselves arguing on the phone about what seemed like trivial matters to Sean but were actually big issues for Angela.

Each was frustrated that they had very little control of their situation and would take out their frustrations on each other during these phone conversations. Angela was worried that their marriage would not last the six months before Sean returned home.

In therapy, Angela and I discussed practical ways to address the situation, and we came up with a plan to Skype with Sean for marital counseling sessions. First, we calculated the time difference (Sean was on a different day), and we agreed on a time to meet. Angela and I sat in a conference room with her iPad propped up so we could see Sean and he could see us. Thank goodness for technology; we were able to meet on approximately a weekly basis and were able to work on the issues in the relationship.

We talked about the couple's history, where they currently were with their relationship, and about their future plans, which included buying a house. There were ups and downs in the sessions, but after many months of hard work, Angela and Sean were reunited in the United States. The couple and their child moved to a Southern state, bought a home, and reported they were doing great now that they were together again. Kudos to them for their hard work and ingenuity!

Because of advances in technology and the fortitude of this couple, we watched a beautiful scenario unfold. Last I heard, the two were thriving in their new home.

## Relief from Anger

I received a call from a man who needed to set up a court-mandated appointment for an anger-management problem. When he came in for the session, he not only told me about the road-rage incident that had involved the police but how his anger issues were beginning to affect his work and home life. My client reported feeling angry his whole life. When I asked him why he was so angry, he said, "I don't know. I'm pissed off all the time."

He talked about getting into fights when he was a kid in school and later, as an adult, the relationships that were lost due to his anger. When asked about his childhood, he indicated he wasn't treated very well by his father and never felt that his father respected him. Later he would admit having feelings of hurt and low self-esteem that were eclipsed by his anger.

We talked about his early childhood "wounds," and I pointed out how sensitive they still were. He agreed and said he'd never really talked about his deeper feelings with anyone before. We both concluded that when he thought he was being disrespected by anyone, the old, unhealed hurt would come flooding back, which then triggered his anger. My client finished his court-mandated anger-management sessions, but stayed in therapy as we discussed this dynamic. He later said that the work we did together helped him feel much calmer.

## Doing the Right Thing

A woman came into my office to talk about the trouble she was having with relationships in her life. From her parents to her boyfriend to her friends, my client wanted to know what was "wrong" with her. She indicated she was surprised that anyone would speak to her. We worked on her communication style, assertiveness, and anger, which seemed to improve as therapy progressed.

During one session, she mentioned she'd had a bad experience after going over her friend's house. The friends were married and had a young child. My client said that when she went to the house, she saw the baby in a dirty diaper, and his parents were inside doing drugs. She was so upset about the baby being neglected that she had to leave. When my client reported this to me, I explained that as a social worker, I was obligated to see that this case was reported to Child Protective Services.

My client initially was afraid to make the call; she did not want to be the person who had this couple's baby taken away from them. I remember turning the discussion around and shifting the focus to the baby, who was reliant on the adults for his care. After a tense session, my client agreed to report what she had seen. This was not easy for her as she worried about losing her friends over this. But after discussing this situation further, my client indicated that she felt good about making the call and believed the baby would be better taken care of in the future.

As with those discussed in the above vignettes, you can have a positive outcome, but you have to reach out and call a therapist first. You have the power to take the positive action that will bring you increased confidence, success, and improved relationships. Calling a therapist can be the first step in fulfilling your goals and dreams and living a more satisfying life. Many people have reported that just making the call brought them a sense of relief.

Hopefully this book will help you make the call *sooner* than later. Call a therapist today!

 # Additional Resources

Relationships

- ⊙ *Getting the Love You Want* by Harville Hendrix, PhD
- ⊙ *The 5 Love Languages* by Gary Chapman

Mindfulness

- ⊙ *The Miracle of Mindfulness* by Thich Nhat Hanh
- ⊙ *The Power of Now* by Eckhart Tolle

Older Adults

- ⊙ *How to Care for Aging Parents* by Virginia Morris

Depression

- ⊙ *The Depression Workbook* by Mary Ellen Copeland
- ⊙ *Mind Over Mood* by Dennis Greenberger, PhD, and Christine A. Padesky, PhD
- ⊙ *The Self-Esteem Workbook* by Glenn R. Schiraldi, PhD

Anxiety

- ⊙ *The Anxiety & Phobia Workbook* by Edmund J. Bourne, PhD

## Stress and Burnout

◉ *The Truth about Burnout* by Christina Maslach and Michael P. Leiter

## Work/Employment

◉ *What Color Is Your Parachute?* by Richard N. Bolles

## Adolescence

◉ *The Self-Esteem Workbook for Teens* by Lisa M. Schab

◉ *Parenting Teens with Love and Logic: Preparing Adolescents for Responsible Adulthood* by Foster Cline

## Substance Abuse

◉ *National Institute on Drug Abuse,* www.drugabuse.gov/publications/drugfacts/understanding-drug-use-addiction

◉ *Substance Abuse and Mental Health Services Administration (SAMHSA),* www.samhsa.gov/find-help/national-helpline

## Existential Angst

◉ *What's Up with My Life? Finding and Living Your True Purpose* by Gail Thackray

◉ *Man's Search for Meaning* by Victor Frankl

## Abuse and Neglect

◉ *The National Domestic Abuse Hotline,* www.thehotline.org

◉ *The National Institute on Aging,* www.nia.nih.gov/health/elder-abuse

◉ *The National Child Abuse Hotline,* www.childhelp.org/hotline

 # Notes

1. Aaron Beck and Gary Emry, with Ruth Greenburg, *Anxiety Disorders and Phobias: A Cognitive Perspective*, USA: Basic Books, 1985.

2. American Psychiatric Association, *Diagnostic and Statistical Manual—V*, desk reference, Washington, DC: American Psychiatric Publishing, 2013.

3. Ibid., 94–95.

4. American Psychological Association, https://www.apa.org/, accessed March 8, 2019.

5. Ibid.

6. Ron Efron-Potter, *Stop the Anger Now*, Oakland, CA: New Harbinger, 2001.

7. Ibid.

8. Timothy Leary, *Turn On, Tune In, Drop Out*, Oakland CA: Ronin Publishing, 1965.

9. Robyn Burton and Nick Sheron, "No Level of Alcohol Consumption Improves Health," *The Lancet*, 392, no. 10152 (2018): 98–988, https://doi.org/10.1016/SO140-6736 (18) 31571-x.

10. Portia Nelson, *There's a Hole in My Sidewalk*, New York, NY: Atria, 2012.

11. Marsha Linehan, *DBT Treatment of Borderline Personality Disorder*, New York: Guilford Press, 1993.

12. Anton Chekov, "Anton Chekhov Quotes," BrainyQuote.com, 2019, accessed March 7, 2019, https://www.brainyquote.com/quotes/anton_chekhov_161769.

13. Herbert Freudenberger with Geraldine J. Richelson, *Burnout: The High Cost of High Achievement*, Harlow, England: Anchor Press, 1980.

14. Amy Cooper Hakim and Muriel Solomon, *Working with Difficult People*, New York, NY: Prentice Hall, 1990.

15. Stephanie Holland and Clare Ward, *Assertiveness: A Practical Approach*, Oxon, United Kingdom: Winslow Press Ltd., 1990.

16. Ibid., 2–5.

17. "You Can't Always Get What You Want," Rolling Stones, *Let It Bleed*, London: Elektra Studios (1969), record.

18. Chris Hansen, "To Catch a Predator," *Dateline NBC*, 2004–2010, MSNBC.

19. American Academy of Pediatrics, (2016), https://www.aap.org/en-us/about-the-aap/aap-press-room/pages/vurtural-violence-impacts-children-on-multiple-levels.aspx.

20. National Coalition Against Domestic Violence, founded 1978, Denver, CO, https://www.thehotline.org/.

21. Mary Kay, "The Truth about Abuse Survey," The Mary Kay Foundation, 2012, content2.marykayintouch.com/public/pws_us/pdfs/company/2012survey.pdf.

22. See Lisa Firestone, "Steps to Overcome Your Critical Inner Voice," *Psychology Today*, May 2010, https://www.psychologytoday.com/us/blog/compassion-matters/201005/steps-overcoming-your-critical-inner-voice), blog.

23. See Robert W. Firestone, "The Fantasy Bond: A Substitute for a Truly Loving Relationship," *Psychology Today*, December 2008, https://www.psychologytoday.com/us/search/site/the %20fantasy%20bond, blog.

24. See *Journal of Religion and Health*, 22 no. 1 (1983): 58–73.

25. Victor Frankl, *Man's Search for Meaning*, Boston, MA: Beacon Press, (2006).

 # My Vision for You

My greatest hope for you is that you will learn to recognize patterns of behavior that are not working anymore as you begin to find more joy in life.

Know that you are deserving of a healthy and successful life and that you can navigate past issues that have become barriers on your path.

You will undoubtedly face some trials and tribulations along the way, but trust that you can make it and do what you want in life. Thank you for going on this journey with me. Please be sure to visit me on my website at www.rciampi.com.

 # Get Help Today

In order to ascertain your level of anxiety, depression, anger, relationship problems, and other debilitating issues, please go to psychology today.com/us/tests for an extensive list of self-tests. Here you can take a free test and have it scored by Psychology Today to gauge your level of discomfort. For a more comprehensive report, a minimal fee will be charged by Psychology Today. This may be a good place to start on your way to wellness.

For clients looking to schedule an appointment with Robert C. Ciampi, LCSW in the northern New Jersey area, a free fifteen-minute telephone consultation will be offered prior to the session. Please be sure to visit me on my website at www.rciampi.com or send me an email at counseling@rciampi.com.

# About the Author

R obert C. Ciampi, LCSW, has worn many hats in his professional career: clinician, therapist, patient advocate, supervisor, consultant, and administrator. He earned a BA in psychology from Montclair State University and he went on to get his MSW at Rutgers University, both in New Jersey. After receiving his licensure as a clinical social worker, he worked in community mental-health centers and hospital settings. As a psychiatric social worker, he provided care for individuals suffering from serious and persistent mental illness as well as patients who were dually diagnosed with mental illness and substance abuse. He went on to work for a behavioral healthcare consulting firm and directed departmental interventions in hospital settings as well as coordinated a program that provided employee-assistance help for staff issues in and outside the workplace. He was also director of inpatient social-work services at the largest hospital in New Jersey. Robert opened a private psychotherapy practice in 2010 and has helped clients with anxiety, depression, stress management, assertiveness training, and many other issues. He also sees clients for couples and marital counseling. Robert enjoys tennis, biking, writing, photography, and skydiving. Robert lives and works in northern New Jersey.